Horary Astrology

An Essential Guide to Astrological Chart Reading, Divination, the Twelve Houses, Planetary Transits, Venus, Mars, Jupiter, Mercury, the Sun, and Moon

© **Copyright 2023 - All rights reserved.**

The content contained within this book may not be reproduced, duplicated, or transmitted without direct written permission from the author or the publisher.

Under no circumstances will any blame or legal responsibility be held against the publisher, or author, for any damages, reparation, or monetary loss due to the information contained within this book, either directly or indirectly.

Legal Notice:

This book is copyright protected. It is only for personal use. You cannot amend, distribute, sell, use, quote or paraphrase any part, or the content within this book, without the consent of the author or publisher.

Disclaimer Notice:

Please note the information contained within this document is for educational and entertainment purposes only. All effort has been executed to present accurate, up-to-date, reliable, and complete information. No warranties of any kind are declared or implied. Readers acknowledge that the author is not engaging in the rendering of legal, financial, medical, or professional advice. The content within this book has been derived from various sources. Please consult a licensed professional before attempting any techniques outlined in this book.

By reading this document, the reader agrees that under no circumstances is the author responsible for any losses, direct or indirect, that are incurred as a result of the use of the information contained within this document, including, but not limited to, errors, omissions, or inaccuracies.

Your Free Gift
(only available for a limited time)

Thanks for getting this book! If you want to learn more about various spirituality topics, then join Mari Silva's community and get a free guided meditation MP3 for awakening your third eye. This guided meditation mp3 is designed to open and strengthen ones third eye so you can experience a higher state of consciousness. Simply visit the link below the image to get started.

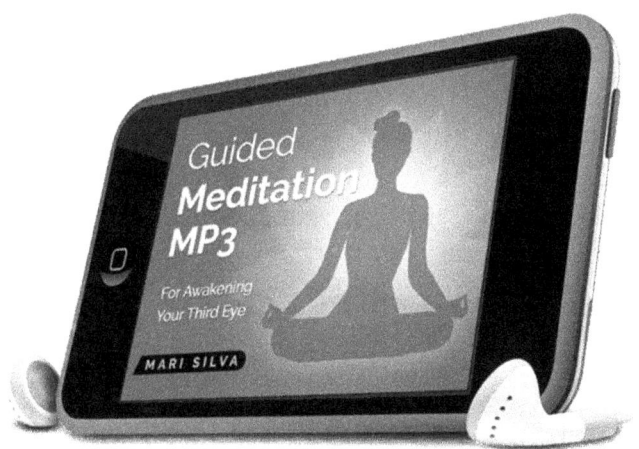

https://spiritualityspot.com/meditation

Table of Contents

INTRODUCTION 1
CHAPTER 1: HORARY ASTROLOGY AND DIVINATION 3
CHAPTER 2: ZODIAC SIGNS BASICS 11
CHAPTER 3: THE DECANS, AN EXTRA LAYER OF MEANING ... 31
CHAPTER 4: 12 ASTROLOGICAL HOUSES AND 2 AXES 41
CHAPTER 5: MAIN CHARACTERISTICS OF THE PLANETS 52
CHAPTER 6: PLANETARY DIGNITIES AND JOYS 68
CHAPTER 7: MAJOR PLANETARY ASPECTS 80
CHAPTER 8: MINOR PLANETARY ASPECTS 89
CHAPTER 9: PLANETARY TRANSITS 99
CHAPTER 10: HOW TO READ ANY HORARY CHART 107
GLOSSARY OF TERMS AND GLYPHS 117
CONCLUSION 123
HERE'S ANOTHER BOOK BY MARI SILVA THAT YOU MIGHT LIKE 125
YOUR FREE GIFT (ONLY AVAILABLE FOR A LIMITED TIME) 126
REFERENCES 127

Introduction

As a branch of ancient astrology, horary astrology has been part of people's lives for thousands of years. As you'll learn from this book, horary astrology is a unique art. It relies on the same principles as other methods of discerning answers based on the position and interaction of heavenly bodies, but it's slightly different. Unlike traditional approaches to astrology, like natal astrology, the horary version is far more straightforward. You only need to know the position of the planets, stars, sun, and moon when asking a particular question to create and interpret a horary chart.

Of course, like other astrology, the zodiac signs are a fundamental part of interpreting your chart. The chapter dedicated to the characters explores them in-depth, thoroughly explaining their characteristics and importance. To accurately use horary astrology for divination, you must pay attention to the decans, which provide additional information associated with your inquiry. Since a specific zodiac sign rules each astrological house, the book has a chapter exploring the individual houses and the 2 axes, which are explained fully later in the book.

You'll learn the fundamental aspects of the planets. Empowered by this knowledge, you'll understand how these heavenly bodies provide accurate answers in horary astrology. The subsequent chapters are dedicated to planetary characteristics called "dignities" and "joys" and the major and minor planetary aspects. It reveals a more in-depth view of how each planet is associated with information seeking. Major and minor planetary aspects embody a unique system of energies, the source of the answer to the querent (one who consults an astrologer). Each planetary aspect has a distinctive role and impact on horary charts. The five principal planetary aspects (the Conjunction, the Sextile, the Square, the Trine, and the Opposition) have the most fundamental role in horary chart interpretation. While minor planetary aspects are less demonstrative than their major counterparts, they should be considered while doing horary divination.

How a planet moves across the sky paints a clearer picture of the querent's sought answer. The penultimate chapter defines the concept of planetary transits and explains how it differs from the aspects. It explores the information transits offer compared to aspects. The last chapter teaches you how to read a horary chart. It provides a beginner-friendly explanation of how horary charts are created, with step-by-step practical instructions and examples of what to consider when doing a horary reading.

If you're ready to embark on the unique and rewarding journey of learning astrological divination, keep reading!

Chapter 1: Horary Astrology and Divination

Astrology is an ancient science studying the influence of heavenly bodies on people's lives. It started thousands of years ago when astrologers and astronomers noticed many of Earth's events are determined by the position of the planets, sun, moon, and stars. Later, it was revealed that how the heavenly bodies were positioned when a person is born could shape their lives by influencing their personality, relationships, and other aspects of life. By identifying the astrological signs that ruled the planets when a person was born, astrologers could get clearer answers about the querent. Other factors, like the astrological houses and angles, affect the outcomes. These factors form an elaborate profile determining a person's life prospects.

Earth's events are determined by the position of the planets, sun, moon, and stars.
https://pixabay.com/es/illustrations/planetas-espacio-tierra-j%C3%BApiter-7612566/

Various past cultures used different astrological practices. Some have evolved, while others have remained the same. Nowadays, you can practice many forms of astrology. For example, you can look into prophecies through modern Western practices, like mundane astrology, interrogatory astrology, the ever-popular natal astrology, and horary astrology.

This first chapter introduces you to horary astrology. You'll learn about its history and position in the vast sea of divinatory practices. You'll be provided with explanations and examples of how this ancient divinatory form works in theory – and in practice.

History and Uses of Horary Astrology

The horary astrology origins can be traced to ancient Sumeria. When describing the art of capturing the moment in the horary chart, the Sumerians used the word "*kairos.*" For them, this term marked the time when the Earth and the heavenly bodies were frozen together, revealing answers related to a particular concern. The question was posed by their astrologers, who could discern the answers by looking up to the heavens.

Horary astrology was popularized in the 17th century by English Astrologer William Lilly, who created several publications about this art. Like many astrologers at the time, Lilly was proficient in medicine, herbology, architecture, and magic. He made astrology available to the masses through his work and publications. In modern times, people rely on natal astrology because they know their time of birth and can afford to pay astrologers for natal charts. However, this was far from the case in the 17th century. So, for people who couldn't afford to pay for complicated natal charts, horary charts represented a more suitable solution. They could receive guidance to resolve their issues and gain answers to burning questions without spending too much money. Lilly popularized the practice of reading the stars based on their current positions. This move was critical for the survival of astrological divination.

Lilly gained knowledge and experience through other astrologers' work who lived and practiced earlier in history. He studied the works of Guido Bonatti, an Italian astrologer who lived before 1300 CE. Bonatti spent much of his life examining the astrological systems created by the ancient Greek, Roman, Sumerian, Egyptian, and Arab civilizations. Bonatti collected the most essential information from these systems, synthesizing them into a system that established the foundation of modern astrology. Lilly translated Bonattis's works (written in Latin) and other astrology-related texts from Greek, Sanskrit, and Near-Eastern languages with cryptic connotations.

William Lilly learned from astrologers and sorcerers who practiced this art in the Middle Ages. Astrology was forbidden due to its association with pre-Christian, pagan belief systems during that time. Despite this, people visited magicians and astrologers to seek guidance in practical matters. Revealing this, Lilly could pinpoint a unique quality of horary astrology - the connection between spirituality and applicable information. Unlike other astrology, horary astrology uses information about the heavenly object to provide information people can use in their current lives. It reminds people that heavenly bodies don't only affect each other in the skies, but they also have a bearing on life on Earth.

Contemporary horary astrology is efficient in answering people's day-to-day concerns. Although nowadays, many don't object to paying for detailed natal charts, they can create their own chart without studying complex planetary associations and links between the zodiac signs and houses.

Another reason people prefer to use horary charts over natal charts is they don't want to learn how the planets will determine their fate. Let's say you want to know if you should apply for a job you're interested in. In this case, you won't care about uncovering how your unique personality traits led to you finding that job. You just want to know whether submitting your application is a good idea.

Besides, not everyone wants to learn about the extensive strengths and weaknesses determined by the positioning and movements of heavenly objects at the time of their birth. Horary astrology provides precise answers without additional information. You must know the exact time of your birth to get answers to similar occurrences in a natal chart. Unlike the date and location of your birth, the time of birth isn't always recorded, even in modern times. So, if you don't know your exact birth time, horary astrology is one of the best ways to seek answers from the stars.

How Is Horary Astrology Used and Why

Horary astrology explores answers to questions based on the inquirer's current situation. The questions must be related to the present to reveal answers of the same nature. They cannot be related to the past or future because that goes beyond the scope of horary astrology. So, instead of asking questions like "Will I succeed in the job offered?" You should ask, "Should I take this job offer?" Similarly, you won't ask, "Was planning to move for a job the right decision?" Instead, ask, "Should I move – to be closer to my new job?"

The interpretation of a horary astrological chart is similar to a birth chart. Once you've asked the question, you can create a chart based on the current standing of the relevant heavenly bodies and interpret their positions to reveal the answer.

The horary chart won't reveal information about situations you've already explored through conscious information seeking. Unlike other divination forms, horary charts won't give you answers from previous lives or the life after this one. They won't offer explanations about death either. You can get answers about certain situations, but the questions must be open-ended. Asking questions requiring a yes or no answer leads to the risk of false results.

Your responses are determined by complex relationships between planetary positions. You shouldn't limit your questions to one-word answers. Even if your inquiry results in a simple answer, seeking information affected by several planetary positions is always better. Novice practitioners are advised to seek prophecies for other people. It takes time to master asking the right questions, let alone creating and reading a horary chart. If a practitioner is determined to seek questions about the future, they should limit their search to up to three months ahead. The planetary positions can determine nothing beyond that at the time of the inquiry. Once created for a specific question, horary charts are valid for three months. You shouldn't ask the same question again within this period; you'll likely get different results. If you do, your results are likely false. Recording the *time of the inquiry* helps you avoid this mistake.

The Connection between Horary Astrology and Divination

Horary astrology is an ancient divination system relying on the same principles as many other future-telling methods. Of course, there are several fundamental differences between horary astrology and other divination forms. The most notable difference is that the former is a passive method. You actively participate in divination when using Tarot cards, runes, and other oracular divination forms. You pick a card, rune, or other tool and engage with them through intuition. With the combined effort of your intuition and the tools chosen, you can get answers to your inquiries. In contrast, horary astrology requires a passive approach because you're essentially looking at the planets to reveal the answers.

Still, there are a few similarities between horary astrology and other divination forms. First, you must explore the concept of divination to understand these. When you perform an act of divination, you're engaging in a seemingly random act. However, in this universe, nothing is coincidental. Your experiences and environment tell you much more about the events you've set in motion with your actions than you're aware of. Every person has a secret history of their life, which is part of a complex energetic network. Engaging in a random act requires the participation of all the forces present in this energy field. As Austrian psychoanalyst Sigmund Freud suggested, people are only aware of a small part of their emotions and thoughts. The rest is hidden in the subconscious, the effects of their thoughts and feelings on their environment and outcomes. Prophetic practices use these forces to reveal the information the practitioner seeks by creating a connection between the subconscious and the energy field surrounding them.

For instance, you're sitting in a restaurant with your friends and want to know what brought you there. The obvious answer might be as simple as one of your friends wanting to celebrate their promotion and inviting you to the restaurant. You decide to dig deeper into the (still conscious) answer. With a little introspection, you may reveal that your recent move to that city is why you're at the restaurant at that specific moment.

When seeking answers through divination, you must understand not all solutions lie in the universe's secret forces. You may not know the answer, but it can become obvious by taking a little time to identify it. For instance, pulling a card from a deck doesn't necessarily mean you were drawn to it because your subconscious was telling you it reveals critical answers. You could have picked it because you knew it had a bent edge - you merely weren't aware of this knowledge.

Horary astrology works the same as other prophecy forms. It extracts information from the energy system by looking at the heavenly bodies in a particular configuration. This configuration is associated with feelings and thoughts and reveals knowledge you otherwise wouldn't have accessed. Using the same example of the restaurant scene, the true answer to your question lies in the planetary configurations at the moment you ask the question. It's like taking a picture of the planets when the thought of questioning why you're at the restaurant comes to mind and freezing the related universe's forces in time. Since these forces are fluid and in constant motion creating a photograph is a way to make them accessible to the conscious mind.

Your natal chart reveals talents, potential, and indications taking the form of actions and thoughts. These are the results of a complex energy process, which astrology (and the divination methods based on it) seeks to explore. Horary astrology focuses on creating a clearer picture. Unlike the natal chart that can change during your life, a horary chart is frozen at that moment. Since the information you gain is based on a particular moment, the astrological symbols are far less fluid.

Horary astrology relies on the same principles as many other astrology forms. One of the most influential aspects of this divinatory practice is the moon's position and characteristics. On a horary chart, as the querent, you are represented by the sign's ruler residing in the first house cusp. Planetary rules of the houses and other aspects determined by the present house cusps crucially impact creating and interpreting horary charts.

Generally, when you read a horary chart, you first appoint your inquiry to a specific house in the chart. For example, if you're looking for a lost animal, you would assign this question to the sixth house, which rules over animals smaller than a goat. On the chart, you'll see this house's cusp residing in a particular sign. A specific planet will rule the sign at that moment. The place of the planet will hold the answer, symbolizing the location of the lost animal. Likewise, the planet's characteristics, determined by the horoscope, will tell you if the missing animal is injured, ill, or in danger. So, the answer to a simple question provides complex results determined by multiple factors. Your inquiry's intention, the intentions of others related to the inquiry, and the options associated with the questions affect your answers.

Horary Astrology at Work

Here is an example of how honorary astrology works in practice:

Charley explained, "I was down with the flu, but I was already making plans for a dinner party I was supposed to hold for my friends the next week, thinking my symptoms would clear up by then. I asked whether I should hold the party on a particular day. However, my chart revealed some unforeseen compilation. It warned me that it's not wise to plan a party because, based on the current planetary position, I was looking for a much longer recovery period than anticipated. I normally don't rush to the doctor with flu-like symptoms, but the warning made me think twice about looking after my health. So, I made an appointment. After some testing, the doctor revealed that I suffered from a serious bacterial infection requiring immediate treatment. I was disappointed to have to cancel my dinner party, but my friends were understanding. And I was grateful for the revelation that saved me from more serious health complications."

As the following testimony suggests, horary charts can reveal answers to questions related to lost objects:

"I was rushing out one winter morning and couldn't find my favorite pair of gloves. They were a birthday present from a dear friend, and I also liked wearing them. I was looking for them in my bag, coat, and closet, thinking I'd put them in either of those places. Since I was in a hurry, I had to settle for another pair before heading out. When I returned home, I decided to look for the gloves again - this time with a little divinatory help. Thinking I'd already looked everywhere else in the house, I asked whether I should look for the gloves in the garage. Based on the planetary chart at the moment of the inquiry, the answer was a clear yes. After going into the garage, I found the gloves. They were on the shelf next to the snow shovel I used the last time I wore the gloves. I took them off, so they wouldn't get dirty while clearing the pathway in front of my home." explained Lewis.

Horary astrology can answer questions on financial matters - as long as they're about you personally:

"When the global pandemic hit, the stock market went into a deep dive. Since I had substantial savings, a friend of mine suggested that I invest it in stock. With the stock prices plummeting, it seemed like a good investment. When the market starts to recover, I could sell my shares for a much higher price. However, I was skeptical about investing my money as I wasn't sure how the economy would fare later on. After consulting the horary chart, I learned that investing in stock was not a good idea, as the market would go further down. I decided against investing, and as it turned out, it was a good decision - the energy crisis caused stock prices to go even lower." Maxine.

Besides answering questions, horary charts can give you clarity over certain situations:

"I recently had a job interview for a position I had coveted for a long time. As time passed, I realized I wouldn't get a call back from the recruiter. I was considering applying for different positions but was hesitant as I was still hoping to get the job I wanted. After consulting the horary chart, I learned that while the recruiter considered me a good fit for the role, the employer didn't, thus giving someone else the position. However, the chart also showed that the person who got the job would soon leave it. About a month later, I received a call from the recruiter asking if I was still interested in the position." Carla.

Chapter 2: Zodiac Signs Basics

You are probably familiar with zodiac signs and have used them to understand your personality and your compatibility with someone or not. However, astrology signs are significantly important in horary astrology, albeit differently. Each zodiac sign brings a different energy to answer your questions.

Wheel of zodiac signs.
https://openclipart.org/detail/326713/vintage-zodiac-wheel-colour

Generally, zodiac signs are the twelve constellations in astrology, called "sun signs" because the sun passes through each one during a specific time of the year. Your sign is determined by the sun's position in the zodiac sign on the day you were born, impacting your personality and life. It can give detailed information about your personality, like your negative and positive traits, mood, relationships, challenges, etc.

In horary astrology, a zodiac sign in your chart can hint at an answer to your question. For instance, if you lose your cell phone and you get Gemini, your phone could be in your office or a place near your office. Since Gemini is the sign of communication, its presence can hint at an answer to communicating or socializing.

Three Types of Signs

1. Cardinal
2. Fixed
3. Mutable

This chapter covers each in detail so you can understand how zodiac signs connect to your horary astrology reading.

Cardinal Signs

The first types are the "cardinal signs," consisting of Capricorn, Libra, Cancer, and Aries. These signs symbolize initiation, innovation, transformation, change, and new experiences, associated with changing seasons. Capricorn is connected to winter, Libra represents the changes in fall, Cancer reflects the warmth of the summer, and Aries is linked to spring. If you get a cardinal sign in your horary reading, it means that this is the best time to take action and make things happen.

Aries

Glyph

Aries glyph represents the ram horns which influence the sign's energy and attitude of taking charge. The ram pushes through and moves everything in its way to achieve its goals. Similar to the ram, Aries is a symbol of strength and drive. People born under this sign are prone to explosive and strong emotions like aggression and losing their temper.

Rams represented new beginnings in ancient cultures.

Keywords

Aries hints at an answer related to any of these traits in a horary reading.

- Impulse
- Impatience
- Bravery
- Straightforwardness
- Determination
- Confidence
- Taking action
- Taking risks
- Boldness
- Passion
- Seeking attention
- Resolution
- Aggression
- Leadership
- Creativity
- Positive energy
- Self-confidence
- Selfishness
- Anger
- Competitiveness

Horary questions could ask about a lost item. If you get Aries in your reading, you'll find what you are looking for in any of these locations.

- On a hill or in a sandy area
- Unfrequented places
- Plastering in the home
- Ceilings

- Roof coverings

Element

Aries' element is fire, which drives the sign's fiery, impulsive, direct, energetic, and curious personality. The fire burning inside an Aries pushes it to fight and lead, providing answers related to fights, arguments, leadership, and promotions.

Modality

As a cardinal sign, Aries has a take-charge personality and prefers to lead rather than follow. Regarding questions about taking the initiative, a modality sign can show you the way.

Ruling Planet and House

Mars is Aries' planet. Mars is the God of War in Roman mythology, making it ideal for the competitive sign willing to win at all costs. It drives their aggression, impulse, and inner fire. Mars represents trouble in your relationships, like conflict and disagreements. Aries belongs to the first house in astrology and provides answers associated with self-worth, appearance, identity, vitality, and self. It indicates the desire to create a union in relationships.

Polarity

Aries has a positive polarity. Positive signs have an outward energy and impeccable self-expression skills. They are compatible with negative polarity signs as opposites attract.

Cancer

Glyph

The cancer symbol is the crab. It reflects its self-protective personality. The glyph can also resemble breasts, symbolizing its mothering and nurturing nature. They often provide answers connected to practicality, spirituality, and empathy.

Keywords

- Imagination
- Intuition
- Sympathy
- Caution

- Shrewdness
- Protection
- Clinginess
- Oversensitivity
- Inability to let go
- Loyalty
- Care
- Moodiness

Vengeance Finding a lost item:
- Kitchens
- Near water or ponds
- Cisterns
- Bathrooms
- Wash houses
- Utility rooms

Element

Cancer is a water sign and reflects the sign's maternal and emotional side. People born under a water element are warm and kind-hearted individuals. These traits make them caring, empathetic, and attached to their partners. A water sign in your horary reading indicates a positive outcome when asking about relationships.

Modality

Cardinal cancer enjoys forming emotional bonds, giving hints to questions about emotions or family relationships. It focuses on the subconscious and creativity.

Ruling Planet and Houses

Cancer is a Moon sign. Like the moon impacts the ocean, Cancer has ebbs and flows or highs and lows of emotions, and their mood changes fast. With relationship questions, a well-placed Moon is a sign that your relationship with your significant other will develop.

Cancer is ruled by the fourth house in astrology, symbolizing foundations, family, and home. It is associated with answers about upbringing and emotional security.

Polarity

Cancer has a negative polarity. Their energy is more receptive and inward, influencing the sign's imaginative, intuitive, and oversensitive personality.

Libra

Glyph

Libra's symbol is the scales. They symbolize Libra's love for balance, harmony, equality, and justice. The glyph can represent the setting sun, reflected in the sign's peaceful, calm, and relaxed personality. Libra provides answers connected to equality and justice.

Keywords

- Art
- Compromise
- Respect
- Indecisiveness
- Likability
- Diplomacy
- Fairness
- Kindness
- Accommodation
- Justice
- Social
- Self-indulgence
- Flirtation
- Gullibility
- Change
- Indecisiveness
- Peace
- Idealism
- Charm

Romance Finding a lost item:
- Closets
- Little houses
- Chambers
- Upper floors
- Barns
- Windmills

Element

Air signs are social butterflies who enjoy freedom and adventure. They often live in their own world but are intelligent and intellectual individuals. Anxious and frequently over-thinkers, they always obsess over the past and what could have been. They hint at answers connected to intellect, socialization, and overthinking.

Modality

Libra is the sign of love and romance, and their cardinal modality drives them to initiate relationships. They can usually provide answers connected to relationships, love, and romance.

Ruling Planet and House

Venus is Libra's ruling planet. Venus is the Goddess of Love and beauty in Roman mythology, traits associated with Libra, who is attractive inside and outside. The planet influences their love for harmony, honesty, commitment, and relationships. Since it's associated with love, Venus, in a horary reading, indicates sweethearts, which is a positive sign if you wonder how your relationship with someone will develop.

Libra falls under the seventh house in the zodiac. It is the house of partnerships but not only romantic; they can also be friendships and business partnerships. If Venus is in your seventh house in a horary reading, the person you ask about is interested in you.

Polarity

Libra's positive polarity influences this social sign's ability to express itself easily.

Capricorn

Glyph

The glyph is an illustration of a sea goat with horns and represents the sign's ability to rise above strong emotions, grow, and go after its goals. It indicates answers related to intense feelings and making dreams a reality.

Keywords

- Humor
- Patience
- Ambition
- Discipline
- Practicality
- Carefulness
- Grudge
- Pessimism
- Sensitivity
- Inner reflection

Self-criticism Finding a lost item:

- Barren fields
- Wood stores
- Cow sheds
- Near thresholds
- Dark places
- Low places

Element

Capricorns are Earth signs, influencing their hardworking and ambitious personality. They have a take-charge personality, so they usually hint at answers connected to leadership and achieving goals.

Modality

The cardinal Capricorns are go-getters who usually plan for the future. This sign can provide answers to questions related to long-term goals.

Ruling Planet and House

Capricorn's ruling planet is Saturn. It symbolizes the sign's determination, responsible, and hardworking nature. This planet hints at answers associated with limitations and learning lessons. Saturn is a symbol for older and mature men in a horary reading.

Capricorn falls under the tenth zodiac house. The sign answers about reputation, status, goals, and career.

Polarity

Capricorns have a negative polarity, and their energy is usually quiet and inward.

Fixed Signs

The second types are the "fixed signs," Aquarius, Scorpio, Leo, and Taurus. As the name indicates, these signs are fixated on their goals and traditions. They are responsible individuals who always finish a project they start. People born under fixed signs are dependable, reliable, loyal, and devoted. They prefer a routine life and struggle with change and disruptions.

Taurus

Glyph

The Taurus symbol is the bull; its glyph is the animal's head with curved horns. Bulls are associated with power, virility, tenacity, stubbornness, and strength. Like their animals, people born under this sign are persistent, hardworking, and never retreat from challenges. This sign will give you answers about power, hard work, and tenacity.

Keywords

- Reliability
- Patience
- Security
- Determination
- Persistence
- Greed

- Resentfulness

Inflexibility Self-indulgence Finding a lost item:
- Stables
- Sheds
- Agricultural outhouses
- Cellars
- Low rooms

Element

Taurus's element is Earth. These individuals are grounded in their beliefs, opinions, and thoughts. It represents practicality and sensibility in a horary reading.

Modality

Fixed Taurus' are materialistic, but they work hard so they can afford the luxurious lifestyle they enjoy.

Ruling Planet and House

Taurus's ruling planet is Venus, the planet of sex, beauty, and money. Venus influences the sign's sensual nature. They eat the best food, dress in the most luxurious clothes, and enjoy spoiling themselves. This sign can provide answers related to commitment and loyalty.

Taurus belongs to the second house, associated with finance, values, and possessions. It can provide guidance with questions associated with money or financial decisions.

Polarity

Taurus has a negative polarity.

Leo

Glyph

Leo's symbol is the lion, influencing their bold, loyal, confident, and playful personality. Its glyph is a lion's tail, mane, and head. The circle represents the sun signifying their strong personalities and presence. Creative, dominant, and confident, Leos can hint at answers connected with high self-esteem and leadership skills.

Keywords
- Faithfulness
- Kindness
- Self-confidence
- Open-mindedness
- Enthusiasm
- Generosity
- Creativity
- Intolerance
- Patronizing

Ego Bossiness Finding a lost item:
- Chimneys
- Places
- Building
- Parks
- Woods

Element

Leo is a fire sign which shows in their warm personalities. They are in touch with their emotional side but prefer to hide their weaknesses and instead show off their strengths to the world. Like fire, they burn with passion.

Modality

Fixed Leos have very powerful personalities, so they prefer to lead rather than follow.

Ruling Planets and Houses

Leo's ruling planet is the Sun. It is impossible not to notice a Leo in a group of people since they shine brightly, just like their ruling planet. They are full of energy and never stop giving. The Sun symbolizes confidence and the development of a relationship in a horary reading.

Leo falls under the fifth house, associated with pleasure. It encourages self-expression, joy, and hobbies. Leo can provide answers connected with having fun and enjoyment.

Polarity

Leo has negative polarity. Their energy is like the sun shining through every part of their being.

Scorpio

Glyph

Scorpio is symbolized by a scorpion. People born under this sign are observant and quiet, but they will not react well if you threaten them. Its glyph is the letter "M" with a tail, symbolic of Scorpio's destructive and creative nature.

Keywords
- Magnetism
- Excitement
- Passion
- Power
- Intuition
- Emotion
- Force
- Determination
- Secretiveness
- Obsessions
- Compulsion
- Resentfulness
- Jealousy
- Courage
- Confidence

Finding a lost item:
- Dare places
- Ruins
- Bathrooms

- Kitchens
- Sinks
- Gutters
- Mudded areas

Element

Scorpio is a water sign. Like the seas and oceans, Scorpio is mysterious and secretive. They struggle with opening up, and you can drown if you try swimming in their deep waters. Scorpio symbolizes hope and a future in a relationship in a horary reading.

Modality

Fixed Scorpios have intense emotions, and their feelings can be stuck because of their inability to open up and express themselves. In a reading, they hint at answers about privacy, secrecy, and lack of self-expression.

Ruling Planets and Houses

Pluto, the farthest planet from the sun, rules Scorpio. It is associated with darkness, representing Scorpio's dark personality. It represents rebirth, death, the subconscious, and intensity. Scorpio can provide answers connected with privacy and the shady side of personalities. It hints that a relationship can have a future in a horary reading.

Scorpio falls under the eighth house, which is associated with psychological processes.

Polarity

Scorpio has a negative polarity.

Aquarius

Glyph

Aquarius' symbol is a water bearer pouring water from a jug. This image represents the streaming of knowledge to quench thirst. The glyph symbolizes two lightning bolts, depicting the sign's limitless perspective; these individuals make their own rules and refuse to live a life dictated by others. Aquarius hints at answers related to standing out, being different, and living life on your terms.

Keywords
- Intellect
- Independence
- Inventiveness
- Originality
- Loyalty
- Honesty
- Friendliness
- Detachment
- Lack of emotion
- Unpredictability
- Creativity

Idealism Intelligence Finding a lost item:
- The upper part of a room
- Roofs
- Attics
- High places
- Hills
- Uneven places

Element

Aquarius is an air sign. They are full of unconventional ideas and don't shy away from sharing with the world. Although clever individuals, their heads are in the clouds. They enjoy new experiences, meeting new people, and visiting new places.

Modality

Fixed Aquarius' are intelligent individuals who value their intellect. They are quirky and unconventional but stand firm by their convictions and beliefs.

Ruling Planet and House

Uranus rules Aquarius and symbolizes individuality, awareness, and innovation. People born under this sign represent these qualities. Uranus encourages them to think differently and develop new ideas. Getting

Uranus is bad news as it represents divorce, separation, and division in relationship questions.

Aquarius falls under the eleventh house, representing hopes, dreams, and friends. It is often referred to as the house of the future. Aquarius is associated with answers related to ideas to improve the future and world.

Polarity

Aquarius is positive polarity.

Mutable Signs

The third types are the "mutable signs," which are Pisces, Sagittarius, Virgo, and Gemini. They are the opposite of fixed signs because they seek chaos and change. They love trying new things and never say "No" to new experiences. People born under this sign are spontaneous and crave variety in their lives.

Gemini

Glyph

Gemini's symbol is the twins. Its glyph is two joined lines, representing neutrality and duality. People born under this sign are communicative, social, restless, and enjoy having fun. Gemini gives answers related to communication.

Keywords

- Communication skills
- Youth
- Eloquence
- Intellect
- Wit
- Inquisition

Inconsistency Superficiality Finding a lost item:

- Paneled rooms
- High places
- Chests

- Communication equipment
- Offices
- Areas near offices

Element

Gemini is an air sign. They enjoy connecting with others and expanding their social network. They always have information to share and participate in idle gossip. Having this sign in your answer signifies socializing and making new friends.

Modality

Mutable Gemini is an expert at collecting and spreading information.

Ruling Planet and House

Gemini's ruling planet is Mercury. Mercury was the messenger of the gods in Roman mythology, which is ideal for the sign that enjoys gossiping and sharing information. It influences the people born under this sign to think and learn. Gemini appearing in an answer hints at intellect and sharing information.

Gemini belongs to the third house, associated with intellect and communication. It influences Gemini to think and develop ideas.

Virgo

Glyph

Virgo's symbol is a virgin maiden. The glyph is the letter "M," with the last part twisting inward, representing modesty and introspection.

Keywords

- Intelligence
- Practicality
- Modesty
- Analysis
- Diligence
- Reliability
- Fuss
- Worry

- Perfection
- Harshness
- Over criticism

Finding a lost item:
- Storage areas
- Studies
- Closets
- Dairy houses
- Barns
- Drawers

Element

Virgo is an Earth sign. They are sensible individuals who take their time before deciding. You'll often get answers related to practicality and planning from a Virgo.

Modality

Mutable Virgo is a skilled individual. They are associated with flexibility and the ability to change.

Ruling Planets and Houses

Virgo's ruling planet is Mercury, the planet of travel, technology, and communication. It influences Virgo's productive, reasonable, and logical nature. The sign hints at answers connected with logic and reason.

Virgo belongs to the sixth house, representing routine, health, responsibility, duty, and service.

Polarity

Virgo has negative polarity.

Sagittarius

Glyph

Sagittarius is symbolized by a centaur, representing this sign's paradoxical and dual personality. Its glyph is an arrow signifying Sagittarius's ability to consistently hit its mark without fail.

Keywords
- Philosophy
- Intellect
- Straightforwardness
- Honesty
- Sense of humor
- Freedom
- Optimism
- Restlessness
- Superficiality
- Irresponsibility
- Carelessness

Finding a lost item:
- Hills
- Stables
- Near radiators or fire
- Upper rooms
- High grounds

Element

Sagittarius is a fire sign. They are hot-headed and the first to take action. They are passionate and assertive individuals who are goal-oriented and make quick decisions. It is often the sign that provides answers related to taking charge and achieving goals.

Modality

Mutable Sagittarius are enthusiastic individuals. Flexibility is key with this sign, and they go with the flow.

Ruling Planet and House

Jupiter rules Sagittarius and symbolizes good fortune, knowledge, and spirituality. It influences the sign's adventurous spirit and desire to see the world. It is associated with answers related to positivity and spontaneity. Sagittarius falls under the ninth house, associated with various qualities such as adventure, wisdom, and knowledge. When Sagittarius is in your reading, it can signify getting out of your comfort zone and trying new things.

Polarity

Sagittarius has a Positive polarity.

Pisces

Glyph

Pisces is represented by fish, and its glyph is of two fish facing different directions. It represents the sign's ability to live in both the real and its own world.

Keywords

- Sympathy
- Intuition
- Selflessness
- Kindness
- Compassion
- Sensitivity
- Imagination
- Gullibility
- Vagueness
- Secrecy
- Idealism
- Escapism
- Dreams
- Creativity

Keywords when you lose an item:

- Fishponds
- Rivers
- Damp areas
- Near wells
- Kitchen

- Bathroom

Element

Pisces is a water sign. These people are deep, emotional, and sensitive. Like the ocean, they have an air of mystery and hold their secrets close to their hearts. They are associated with answers about imagination, privacy, and dreams.

Modality

Mutable Pisces are dreamers with a vision for themselves and the future.

Ruling Planet and House

Pisces's ruling planet is Neptune, the god of the seas in Roman mythology. The planet symbolizes spirituality, imagination, and dreams. It is associated with answers about fantasy, dreams, and deep emotions. It hints at answers connected with self-deception, deceit, and relationship confusion.

Pisces belongs to the twelfth and last house of the zodiac. It represents seclusion and mysticism.

Polarity

Pisces has negative polarity.

The more you learn about zodiac signs and their characteristics, the more you understand horary astrology and find answers to your questions. Everything each sign represents can relate to an answer in a horary reading.

Chapter 3: The Decans, an Extra Layer of Meaning

Decans, called "faces" or "decanates," are unique astrological factors in horary astrology. Therefore, they should be considered during horary divination. The 360 degrees of the zodiac wheel is divided into 36 segments - each corresponding to a decan or segment, splitting each zodiac sign into three parts. Each decan occupies 10 degrees on the zodiac wheel and adds unique meaning to the traits, situations, and outcomes determined by a particular zodiac sign.

Each decan occupies 10 degrees on the zodiac wheel.
https://pixabay.com/es/illustrations/astrolog%c3%ada-simbolos-acuario-aries-6808362/

How to Identify the Decans on a Horary Chart

Over the history of the practice, people identified decans on astrological charts in many ways. The most popular approach associated with horary divination is the triplicity method. It splits each sign into thirds and assigns heavenly bodies to them. The association is made based on the traits of other signs with the same triplicity. According to this, the first 10 degrees of each zodiac sign belongs to the sign's fundamental characteristics. The second 10 degrees are linked to the next sign in the zodiacal wheel with the same element or triplicity. The last 10 degrees are associated with a third sign with the same triplicity.

Here is a list of decans on the astrological chart based on this method:

Aries
- 1st decan - 0-9 degrees
- 2nd decan - 10-19 degrees
- 3rd decan - 20-29 degrees

Taurus
- 1st decan - 0-9 degrees
- 2nd decan - 10-19 degrees
- 3rd decan - 20-29 degrees

Gemini
- 1st decan - 0-9 degrees
- 2nd decan - 10-19 degrees
- 3rd decan - 20-29 degrees

Cancer
- 1st decan - 0-9 degrees
- 2nd decan - 10-19 degrees
- 3rd decan - 20-29 degrees

Leo
- 1st decan - 0-9 degrees
- 2nd decan - 10-19 degrees
- 3rd decan - 20-29 degrees

Virgo
- 1st decan - 0-9 degrees
- 2nd decan - 10-19 degrees
- 3rd decan - 20-29 degrees

Libra
- 1st decan - 0-9 degrees
- 2nd decan - 10-19 degrees
- 3rd decan - 20-29 degrees

Scorpio
- 1st decan - 0-9 degrees
- 2nd decan - 10-19 degrees
- 3rd decan - 20-29 degrees

Sagittarius
- 1st decan - 0-9 degrees
- 2nd decan - 10-19 degrees
- 3rd decan - 20-29 degrees

Capricorn
- 1st decan - 0-9 degrees
- 2nd decan - 10-19 degrees
- 3rd decan - 20-29 degrees

Aquarius
- 1st decan - 0-9 degrees
- 2nd decan - 10-19 degrees
- 3rd decan - 20-29 degrees

Pisces
- 1st decan - 0-9 degrees
- 2nd decan - 10-19 degrees
- 3rd decan - 20-29 degrees

Interpreting the Zodiac Signs Decans

Aries

Decan 1 - Ruled by Mars, the Aries' faces are impulsive actions, ambitions, passion, and relentless pursuits. In divination, it could mean you'll develop innovative ideas, face your challenges without fear, and be outspoken about your desires. It embodies the typical characteristic of Aries - the action-oriented sign that never slows down. You must learn to take a softer approach to life. Otherwise, you'll always let your negative emotions lead you instead of being the leader you desire to be.

Decan 2 - Governed by the Sun, this decan indicates a more sensual and fluid lifestyle. This face has the bold confidence of the Aries signs and the natural optimism leading to passionate pursuits. Despite this, you'll still be restless deep down. You feel you can achieve more. In divination, this decan depicts creative pursuits and the desire to catch the eye of those around you.

Decan 3 - Under the reign of Venus, the third face of Aries indicates independence, bossy behavior, and lots of good luck. If this decan arises in your horary chart, it indicates that you are probably occupied with something that inspires you. Or, you may opt for traveling and engaging in nomadic pursuits.

Taurus

Decan 1 - Governed by Mercury, the first face of Taurus is all about aesthetics. As a typical Taurus, while ruled by this sign, you'll be charming, sociable, and ready to speak your mind - although you may come off as slightly materialistic. When this face appears on the horary chart, you'll strive for predictability and show loyalty in your relationships. Your senses are heightened, enabling you to find the smartest way to resolve your problems.

Decan 2 - Headed by the Moon, this decan reflects the need for perfection. You'll communicate your desires to larger groups and be very detailed. In horary divination, this face of the Taurus indicates that you may come off as too rigid or calculated in others' eyes during your inquiry. Being more helpful would help you to avoid issues.

Decan 3 - Ruled by Saturn, this decan showcases practical and reliable pursuits. You'll be determined to show off your loyalty and seriousness about your relationships. Fortunately, you'll be successful, but you probably already know this. You're following the same path that led you to past success for a reason. You may come into money or have other achievements.

Gemini

Decan 1 - Under Mercury's rule, this decan reflects a period of quick thinking and extravagant, sociable behavior. You'll be flexible and ready to talk about anything, albeit unable to focus on one subject for long. Showing characteristics of a typical Gemini sign, this is the time to enjoy what the world offers. However, don't be surprised if your behavior causes conflict with those preferring a more peaceful life.

Decan 2 - Governed by the planet Venus, the second face of Gemini is more expressive and charming. In horary divination, it can indicate that you'll seek attention by expressing your opinions. You'll strive to absorb as much knowledge as needed to obtain your goals. This face denotes a more conflict-averse behavior, although you must be careful with whom you form relationships.

Decan 3 - Ruled by Uranus, this face showcases open-minded behavior. It denotes the opportunity to apply your out-of-the-box thinking skills. You'll be optimistic, creative, adventurous, and ready to help others, even if the only thing you can do is listen to their problems. You may feel rebellious, especially if your independence or social status is threatened.

Cancer

Decan 1 - Governed by the Moon, the first face of Cancer denotes emotional and intuitive behaviors. In horary divination, this decan means you'll be connected to your intuition, prompting you to make good decisions and avoid conflicts. You'll nurture your talents, relationships, and those around you. It can indicate an emotional period. Depending on the nature of the emotions, your life can change in either direction.

Decan 2 - Under Pluto's rule, the second decan of Cancer is far more practical and suggests the need for deep considerations. You may be more stubborn and sentimental than usual in the upcoming period. Yet the same qualities allow you to care for yourself and others. Pay attention to the negative aspects of this decan, including the possessive and brooding behaviors, and change them as soon as you notice them.

Decan 3 - Headed by Neptune, this decan is about fantasy and connecting to your subconscious desires. You may be harboring romantic or dreamy illusions, and now it's time to act on them. In horary divination, this face can signify you'll forgive someone who has hurt you.

You may deepen your spirituality to find peace and move past your hurts.

Leo

Decan 1 - Ruled by Saturn, this decan is a harbinger of a bright and playful period. However, it can indicate you'll be prideful and may need to keep your ego in check. You'll place a high emphasis on your appearance and reputation. Still, in a horary chart, this decan is considered a good sign as it denotes loyalty to your loved ones and sensitivity to their needs.

Decan 2 - Governed by Jupiter, the second face of Leo is a sign of positive things to come. You'll enjoy your freedom, rebelling against rules, and be ready to have the time of your life. You'll seek attention by reaching out to others, seeking to entertain and connect with them. You may accompany someone on their travels and offer them great ideas or performances they're sure to enjoy.

Decan 3 - Under Mars's rule, the last face of Leo is more daring and aggressive than the previous one. This decan represents stubborn behavior, passion, and kindness toward others in horary astrology. You'll follow through on any mission because you'll be forever optimistic about the outcome. Depending on the nature of your inquiry, you may be driven by larger goals forcing you to take a leadership position.

Virgo

Decan 1 - Ruled by the magnificence of the Sun, the first decan of Virgo represents the true nature of this sign. It is the face of a detail-oriented, ambitious, and ever-so-practical sign. In horary divination, it indicates a period obsessed with self-improvement. You'll have trouble with criticism and messy situations. Still, you'll be reliable and always ready to help those in need.

Decan 2 - Governed by Saturn, this face shows a more stand-offish and materialistic side of Virgo. It indicates a fierce determination to follow through with plans and focus on the bigger picture. Despite being honed on in your tasks, you'll still have time to please those around you - mainly because you know they can bring you closer to your goals and cover you with the praise your strive for.

Decan 3 - Under Venus's rule, the last face of Virgo is more whimsical and artistic. It indicates you'll exhibit mature behaviors and be generous, warm-hearted, and loving with those around you. Unlike this sign's previous faces, this one seeks attention. It can signify you'll be more likely to be shy about enjoying sensuality. You'll have no trouble expressing your creativity by improving your aesthetics.

Libra

Decan 1 - Ruled by Venus, this decan indicates your need to make a statement in life. You'll seek luxury, love, and beauty. Whatever you obtain, you'll guard jealously, although you do not wish to engage in conflicts. You'll aim for balance by helping others attain the same goals. Be careful, as you may struggle to remain grounded, particularly in an unstructured environment.

Decan 2 - Under Uranus's rule, the second face of Libra is about fighting the status quo. It denotes wanting to be original in horary astrology. This decan indicates you'll be determined to create unique ideas and stand out from the crowd. Unlike the typical Libra sign, this face is more rebellious. It focuses more on the big picture rather than getting along with others.

Decan 3 - Governed by Mercury, this decan suggests a socialization period. You'll seek to balance your life, mediate conflicts, and entertain others. You'll be a free spirit, happy to make new acquaintances, but also a little vain. You'll likely keep your mind busy, and if you can't find company to help you stay engaged, a good book will do equally well.

Scorpio

Decan 1 - Ruled by Pluto, this decan presents a dependable and loyal mindset. You'll be committed to your goals and others. During this time, you're unlikely to change your mind. You'll leave little room for misinterpretation of your thoughts and emotions. However, you may have periods of dark brooding preventing you from connecting to people. These moments will be more about inner transformation than anything else.

Decan 2 - Governed by Neptune, the second face of Scorpio is a selfless yet moody and impatient sign. In horary, this decan indicates periods of daydreaming, and you'll take everything lightly. It can suggest you're becoming sensitive to energetic influences and less centered. While having your head in the clouds may not benefit your long-term goals, you can use this time to give in to your artistic urges.

Decan 3 - Under Moon's rule, this is the most intuitive and sensitive face of the Scorpio sign and the most popular. You'll be seen as a nurturing person, always ready to be there for those in need. You'll have great empathy for others' feelings, yet be cunning enough to protect yourself and your loved ones from being swept away by other people's problems.

Sagittarius

Decan 1 - Governed by Jupiter, this decan showcases the typical Sagittarius sign. It shows optimism and an independent and adventurous spirit. Horary divination indicates that although non-committal, you'll be lucky in many areas of life. You'll strive to cherish your independence by staying open-minded and curious about new ideas for making it on your own. You may seek new adventures and knowledge.

Decan 2 - Headed by Mars, the second face of the Sagittarius sign is far more disciplined, loyal, and dependable than its predecessor. However, it indicates you'll be action-oriented and likely to take a more aggressive approach. The latter can seem controlling. Fortunately, you'll know how to make up for it with humor. You'll seek new ways to express yourself and succeed in competitions.

Decan 3 - Ruled by the Sun, the last decan of this sign is the freest. Depending on the context of your inquiry, it can indicate you'll meet new people, make an impulsive decision, or create new experiences. You may be focused on your appearance and social status and seek to charm everyone you meet. Your ability to express yourself creatively will help you with the latter.

Capricorn

Decan 1 - Ruled by Saturn, this decan highlights the textbook Capricorn characteristics - old-fashioned and glamorous thinking, occasionally laced with impatience. You'll seek a distinguished status and won't let any grueling task, challenging goal, or your goals stop you. However, you'll make your own rules, which can come off as disrespectful. Your aspiration to have a structured life can be your biggest weapon to obtain success.

Decan 2 - Being governed by Venus, the second face of the Capricorn sign is far friendlier than the first. It denotes you'll be agreeable, enthusiastic, and energetic, albeit a little too proud of yourself. You'll likely seek sensual and hedonistic pursuits and enjoy the beauty of life by finding balance in everything. You'll work hard, but have plenty of rest, too.

Decan 3 - Headed by the planet Mercury, this decan is mysterious yet curious, vibrant, and endlessly thoughtful. This period indicates you'll be curious, helpful, and tender-hearted. People will turn to you with their problems without the risk of being judged, and you'll only care about the truth, not the reasons someone fell off track.

Aquarius

Decan 1 - Under Uranus's rule, the first face of the Aquarius sign indicates defiance and making radical yet innovative moves. You give in to artistic pursuits; some may even make you look eccentric. However, soon others will follow your example and fully support you. You'll have a vision for making the world a better place. You may struggle with restrictions and reclaim your independence.

Decan 2 - Governed by Mercury, the second face of this sign is rather versatile. Sometimes it indicates you'll be restless and seek your own intellectual stimulation. At other times, it symbolizes a social butterfly who enjoys communicating with others and is fulfilled by endless conversations. You may come up with great ideas to sell to anyone or advice people will listen to.

Decan 3 - Ruled by Venus, this decan is the most affectionate face of Aquarius. It indicates a period of good judgment and aspirations for autonomy and balance. Your romantic side will flourish, and you'll have no trouble fitting in with like-minded people. Unlike the sign's previous two decans, this one is more about following trends than creating them. Still, you'll prioritize the beautiful parts of life.

Pisces

Decan 1 - Governed by Neptune, the first face of the Pisces sign denotes friendly, kind, and devoted behavior. You are likely to be creative and use your imagination to its fullest. You'll harbor tender, romantic aspirations and become concerned with hypothetical situations. The decan warns you to occupy yourself with creative pursuits to avoid over-romanticizing people and experiences, allowing you to give in to creativity while remaining grounded in reality.

Decan 2 - Headed by the Moon, this decan symbolizes independence and genuine aspects of the Pisces sign. You can expect an emotional period with unpredictable turns. You'll keep your personal space protected and remain reclusive for the moment. Despite this, you'll maintain your well-being and that of your loved ones. You'll have a chance to listen and care for others.

Decan 3 - Under Pluto's rule, the last face of the twelfth sign is the embodiment of empathy and exceptional listening skills. However, your thoughts and emotions will remain secretive and mysterious. You will likely make a good impression by persisting with your goals and taking on challenging tasks. This decan can symbolize necessary alone time.

Chapter 4: 12 Astrological Houses and 2 Axes

Since a specific zodiac sign rules each astrological house, this chapter helps you to explore them. The illustration of the zodiac wheel with the astrological houses, the IC-MC (Imum Coeli - Medium Coeli) axis, and the AC-DC (Ascendant - Descendant) axis represents the frame of a horary chart. This wheel is split into four quadrants, adding another layer of meaning to the interpretation of the houses. The houses in the first quadrant are associated with drive and motivation. The houses in the second quadrant are linked to instinct and intuition. The houses in the third quadrant are the embodiment of knowledge and thinking. The houses in the fourth quadrant are tied to a person's being or existence. The chapter discusses the axes and their significance in horary divination.

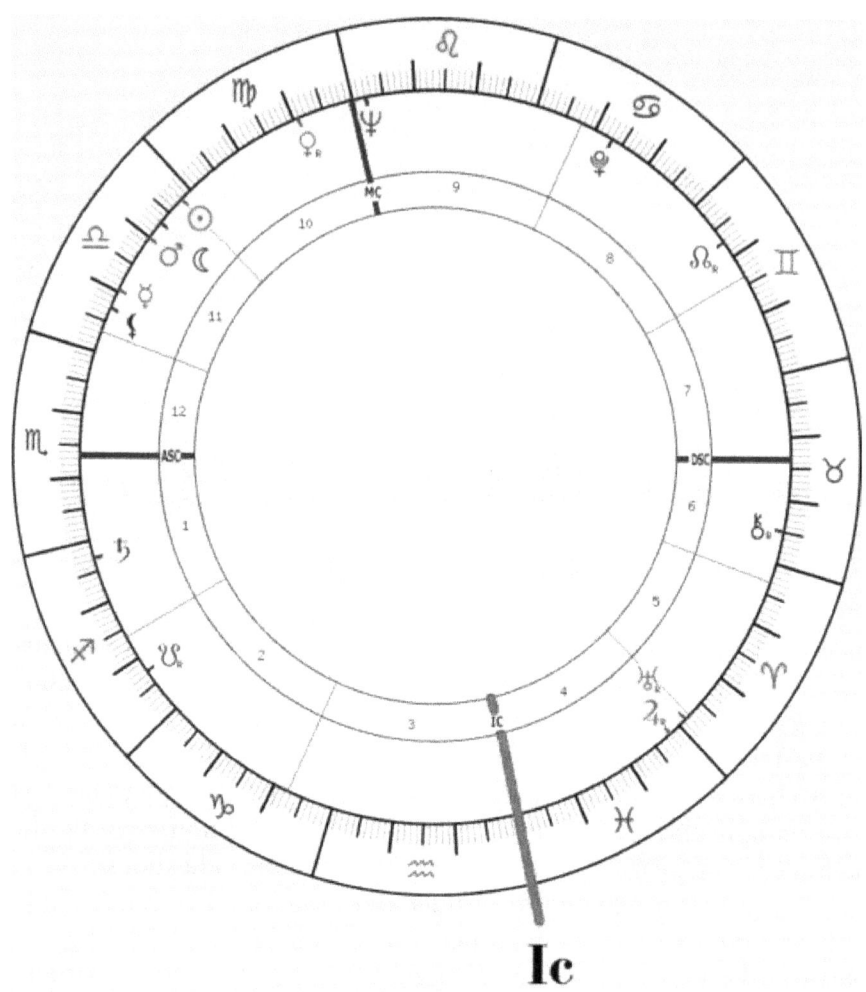

The axis on the wheel.
Coddod, CC BY-SA 4.0 <https://creativecommons.org/licenses/by-sa/4.0>, via Wikimedia Commons https://commons.wikimedia.org/wiki/File:Imum_Coeli_Bearzot.png

The 12 Houses

1st house

Zodiac sign: Aries

Keywords: Health, life, body.

Correspondences: Eyes, head, life-changing events, and red.

Ruling planet: Mars - suggesting a strong sense of self and ego-driven decisions.

It can answer questions about yourself, including your body image and physical appearance, mental health, and overall fitness and vitality.

This house is the domain of first impressions, your image, and your appearance. It can signal you'll be ready to make a fresh start after a bad experience. Pay attention to the surrounding information, as the event you'll need to recover from might still happen; it's not an event from the past. It could be an accident or health event you'll struggle to overcome. Besides the new start for yourself, the house can reveal something about your relatives' lives. You may spend time with your grandparents, nieces, nephews, or grandchildren and learn about their personalities.

Mars in this house is weak in Sagittarius and Pisces and strong in Virgo and Gemini.

2nd house

Zodiac sign: Taurus

Keywords: Finances, livelihood, items, movable possessions.

Correspondences: Bright green color, events in professional life, neck, and shoulders.

Ruling planet: Venus - indicating unique values.

It can answer questions about finances, movable possessions (including clothes, vehicles, and other items), and allies (business partners or lawyers).

Due to Taurus's strong influences, the second house is linked to your material possession, income, financial status, and environment. It can refer to an experience you'll receive through your senses or something you'll see, taste, smell, touch, or hear. If you struggle with a self-esteem issue, you'll have a chance to get a confidence boost. You may get a promotion or acknowledgment for your hard work. Or you may be able to afford to buy something you've wanted for a long time. On the other hand, the house can bring bad news about financial losses and a close relative's health.

Venus in this house is strong in Taurus, Libra, and Pisces and weak in Aries, Virgo, and Scorpio.

3rd house

Zodiac sign: Gemini

Keywords: Neighbors, siblings, journey, spiritual exploration.

Correspondences: The nervous system, hands, throat, lungs, breath, social events, and yellow.

Ruling planet: Mercury - highlighting communication in relationships with yourself and others.

It can answer questions about your siblings, other relatives, neighbors, and others in your neighborhood, roommates, and people you have met online. It can reveal information about early education, traveling, and contracts.

Under the chatty Gemini's rule, the third house governs all interactions. In Horary astrology, this signals you'll be actively communicating in person and on mobile devices. Whether this communication occurs in a school, neighborhood, or another place, you'll get your point across efficiently. You may be signing new contracts with recent acquaintances or receiving packages or deals. Sometimes, you'll have to deal with rumors and gossip generated by or related to your family, friends, or community.

Mercury in this house is weak in Sagittarius and Pisces and strong in Gemini and Virgo.

4th house

Zodiac sign: Cancer

Keywords: Building, home, land, parents.

Correspondences: White and silver, events at home or the family, the chest area, and the stomach.

Ruling planet: The Moon - indicating the connection to home.

It can answer questions about your family and parents (more precisely, your father). Or you can gain resolution for issues about immovable possessions (house, land, or other fixed property).

Governed by Cancer, the fourth house represents a good basis for all planetary and sign aspects. You may receive surprising information about your home, security, or privacy. If you have elderly or ill parents or children, you may receive bad news about them. Or your role as a caretaker of your children will be threatened by income loss. You may need a little TLC because you've been too harsh lately. Sometimes, the house will relate to a family member's finances or conflict and provide a possible resolution for putting things to rest.

The Moon in this house is strong in Taurus and Cancer and weak in Scorpio and Capricorn.

5th house

Zodiac sign: Leo

Keywords: Sex, children, game, gambling, please.

Correspondences: Gold, joyful events, the heart, the upper back, and the spine.

Ruling planet: The Sun - linked to the pleasurable side of life.

It can answer questions about your relationships with your children, sentiments about having children, or the childish behavior of others. It can reveal information about romance, sex, hobbies, and gambling.

The fifth house is headed by Leo, the most dramatic sign of the zodiac. It relates to creative and fun experiences. You may get to express your creativity through hidden or existing talents. This house in horary is the sign of colorful experiences to come or possible romance on the horizon. Sometimes, you may receive surprising news about your children (or future children), lovers, and hobbies. The house can relate to your person as someone's child, meaning you'll receive information about your mother and father (possibly about their deaths or finances).

The Sun in this house is strong in Aries and Leo and weak in Libra and Aquarius.

6th house

Zodiac sign: Virgo

Keywords: Illness, injury, litigation, open enemies, servants, and small animals.

Correspondences: The abdominal area, digestive system, spleen, stressful events, and dark green and brown.

Ruling planet: Mercury - suggesting a link to physical and mental health.

It can answer questions about illness, injuries, accidents, health in general, and small animals. It can reveal information about your place of work and relationships with co-workers and hired employees, including those you employ for one-time jobs (like professionals for specific projects in your home).

The sixth house is the center of health, property, and service. Under the communicative Mercury's rule, the house governs professions thriving on schedules, organization, helpfulness, routines, and serving others. If you have relatives or friends working in medicine, the army, or the police among your close acquaintances, the message from this house may be about them. You can expect changes if you have pets and property owned by you or a family member. Or, if you're about to embrace a healthier, natural lifestyle, you may receive guidance about a suitable diet and exercise plan.

Mercury in this house is weak in Gemini and Virgo and strong in Sagittarius and Pisces.

7th house

Zodiac sign: Libra

Keywords: Partners, spouses, marriage.

Correspondences: Light blue and pink, events related to romantic life, the lower back area, kidneys, butt, and skin.

Ruling planet: Venus - linked to romantic and business relationships.

It can answer questions about feelings and bonds in relationships and marriage. You can learn about the intricacies of other partnerships, including business connections and adversaries from your personnel or professional life.

The seventh house represents the home of relationships and connections to other people. This house can bring you news about your romantic or business relationships in horary. You may seal that business deal you've been working on lately or sign a contract with a new client or partner. Changes in your relationship dynamics or marriage (current or previous) may force you to take legal action. Sometimes, it will be about your existing legal matters, including court battles against someone who committed a crime against you or your loved ones.

Venus in this house is weak in Aries, Virgo, and Scorpio and strong in Taurus, Libra, and Pisces.

8th house

Zodiac sign: Scorpio

Keywords: Death, inheritance, debt, fear, illness, and other people's finances.

Correspondences: The hips, reproductive system, deaths, other mournful events, and black.

Ruling planet: Pluto - indicating a strong association with death and sex.

It can answer questions about shared resources you can or will have access to. For example, you can learn about inheritance, grants, tax returns - and debts you must pay. It can reveal information about your partner's finances and fears about death.

Often called the weak house, the zodiac's eighth house is shrouded in mystery. It governs birth, death, transformation, secretive forces, sex, shared energies, and bonds. You might receive bad news about your or your partner's finances or health or suffer their loss due to death or betrayal. In contrast, the information revealed by this house may be about an upcoming financial benefit. With Pluto's energy comes death, but with death often comes renewal energy like an inheritance to ease your hardship. On the other hand, if you owe someone, they may be ready to collect their dues, which further diminishes your self-worth.

9th house

Zodiac sign: Sagittarius

Keywords: Travel, being abroad, foreign people and experiences, wisdom, teachers, spirituality, and religion.

Correspondences: Purple, events about travel and foreign cultures, the liver, thighs, and legs.

Ruling planet: Jupiter - a powerful link to spirituality and knowledge.

It can answer questions about long-distance relationships and travel plans, especially if these involve foreign lands or cultures. It can provide guidance regarding higher education, learning options, material (including books you can learn from or which university or college to choose), religion, teachers, philosophy, spirituality, and books.

Under the ever-inspired Sagittarius's rule, the ninth house is the embodiment of the open mind. In horary divination, this house opens a world of possibilities. Ensure you consider how it relates to your questions. You can discover new adventures, from travel to foreign languages to education to adopting a new religion or code of conduct. Whatever you do, it's guaranteed you'll stay motivated and optimistic about where your path leads. This house is likened to luck, but you may need to take some risks to attract it. Sometimes, it will be about second-degree family members (including grandchildren and in-laws), professors, or publishers.

Jupiter is weak in Gemini, Virgo, and Capricorn and strong in Cancer, Sagittarius, and Pisces.

10th house

Zodiac sign: Capricorn

Keywords: Career, action, work, reputation, and employers.

Correspondences: Gray and brown, promotions and other positive work events, the joints, skeletal system, and teeth.

Ruling planet: Saturn - suggesting ambition and perseverance.

It can answer questions about your career, property, public image, or your partner's property or image. It can help you explore your relationship with authority figures (including law enforcement and government) and your mother.

The tenth house is particularly institutionalized, not surprising since it's ruled by the natural-born achiever Capricorn. Like its ruling sign, the house shows relevance in structures, tradition, achievements, rules, awards, and discipline. It can be a harbinger of fame, the rise of a public image, or the signal you'll make an authority figure you admire (like your father or boss) proud. This house is linked to your professional life and career, reflecting your effort to present your desired image. Sometimes, it can be associated with an authority figure's health, your health, or your child's health.

Saturn is strong in Libra, Capricorn, and Aquarius and weak in Aries, Cancer, and Leo.

11th house

Zodiac sign: Aquarius

Keywords: Hope, good fortune, wishes, friendships.

Correspondences: Blue, lucky events, the circulatory system, shins, calves, and ankles.

Ruling planet: Uranus - associated with relationships with friends and acquaintances.

It can answer questions about getting along with friends and communities and reveal how to make your hopes and wishes come true. You can learn about forming alliances or whether you should join certain memberships and groups.

The eleventh house governs fortune and wishes in relationships about humanitarian causes, networking, friends, and other social groups. It can show you if you'll be susceptible to rebellion against society's rules or remain the team player you currently are. Ruled by the highly sociable

Aquarius, this house can be about making connections with large groups of people or catering to their desires through technology, social media, or other platforms. You may seek innovative ideas, surprising luck, and eccentric behavior. The house is linked to money you inherit from your mother's side, a close family member's health, and new additions to the family (including through marriage, adoption, or foster care).

12th house

Zodiac sign: Pisces

Keywords: Imprisonment, exile, hidden enemies, large animals, black magic.

Correspondences: The lymphatic system, feet, sudden events, and light green.

Ruling planet: Neptune - Implying that the house is associated with secrets, fears, and mystery.

It can answer questions about hidden, mysterious, or fearsome and clinically sounding places, including prisons, retreats, hospitals, and monasteries. You can get resolutions related to a recent loss, people who secretly want you to fail, large animals, or things you do to undermine yourself.

This house represents the final phase of the process. It's about tying up loose ends and marking endings (in old age and projects). However, it can be about beginnings, the afterlife, dreams, and artistic pursuits. It can be a sign it's time to surrender to the changes brought by the end and await the renewal. Sometimes, this house can denote isolation and hidden or cold places where people usually feel isolated. It doesn't necessarily mean you'll end up in prison, a hospital, or a similar institution. It means you're unaware of a close person's isolated (hidden) intentions.

The Two Axes and Their Four Points

The two axes in the horary chart represent the connection between 4 crucial points of the astrological wheel. These are the Ascendant and the Descendant (connected with the AC-DC axis), the Imum Coeli, and the Midheaven (linked with the IC-MC axis).

The Ascendant (AC) and the Descendant (DC) are at opposite ends of a horary chart. The former lies at the beginning of the first house, while the latter is positioned at the cusp of the seventh house. The AC-

DC axis ties two contradictory forces or aspects of life together.

At the verge of the House of Self, the Ascendant is the domain of personal traits and perceptions. It showcases qualities you can objectively see and accept in yourself. Most people are proud of these and happy to show them off. The AC represents the center of a person's planetary characteristics and is often driven by the person's ego. Due to this, it will always be a constructed image. How you wear your hair, dress, makeup, how you hold your body, and your facial expressions reflect this desire to show a particular picture. While this may make people think they know who you are, they only get what you want to show them. It's like a mask of traits you believe will make you more desirable and accepted.

The Descendant shows the other side of the story. It is the cusp of the 7th house of relationships and hidden qualities. The DC is linked to what lies in the shadow of your perfectly constructed image - the traits you dislike about yourself and refuse to accept. Many people have characteristics they ignore, repress, or disassociate from, just to conform to their relationships. The latter is the theme of the 7th house and is a massive driving force shaping people's lives. However, no matter how irritated by the traits, you refuse to acknowledge them and are still drawn to them. Mostly you'll be attracted to people with these characteristics. The culprit is the AC-DC axis. In horary astrology, this axis reminds you of connections you can't deny. As your relationship deepens, everybody you meet during the rule of the 7th house will notice your true self even if you can't. You can unveil your shadow self by studying your relationships with others and observing your behavior through other people's perspectives. Working with the horary chart by asking questions about your relationships can help you realize your true self.

The role of the AC-DC axis is to create the balance necessary for your overall well-being. The 1st house isn't only about appearance; it's also about physical and mental health. Your health enormously impacts your ability to establish good relationships and vice versa. You inevitably attract people who are more like your descendant and create relationships with them, improving your quality of life. By bringing these two aspects together, elevate yourself and grow into someone who doesn't rely on others for acceptance but can stay true to yourself.

As the cusp of the 4th house, the Imum Coeli is associated with family, home, and other foundational aspects of life. If you are around your IC on your horary chart, you can expect to see the ruling planet's effect on your environment. You'll see them in your home, those your share your environment with, and your feelings about your living arrangements. The IC affects how you feel about a place you've just moved into, whether you're ready to settle in one place or what you consider home. It can affect your perception of your past environment - how you grew up, your experience in your environment, and much more.

The Midheaven (MC) is the cusp of the 10th astrological house. It showcases your sentiments and thoughts about your career, reputation, and social standing. The MC is responsible for the impression you leave on people who haven't met you but have heard about your accomplishments. It's infused with the traits of the ruling planet, allowing these to seep into your professional and public profiles. Different aspects of the ruling matters can affect your professional life, effectively including other people's opinions about you in your work environment. You typically won't be aware of this influence unless you look into the IC-MC connection on the horary chart. In horary, the IC- MC axis represents the link between home and work - two interconnected aspects balancing your life. Together, they represent your legacy, left by the ancestors who worked very hard for their achievements. These can be long-lost ancestors or even your parents. In some cases, the linkage is related to you as a parent.

Chapter 5: Main Characteristics of the Planets

The characteristics of planets in horary astrology are often confusing for beginners. However, understanding and recognizing the significance of each can go a long way toward improving your predictive accuracy. Every planet has its special meaning and effects when it appears in a chart, from Mars representing strength and ambition to Saturn representing responsibility and tradition. Navigating these different qualities is key to accurately analyzing how the planetary movement will affect someone's life. This chapter explains each planet's significance, offering insight into their meaning in practice and how to understand their movements and how they interact with each other.

Planets and Their Significance in Horary Astrology

Sun

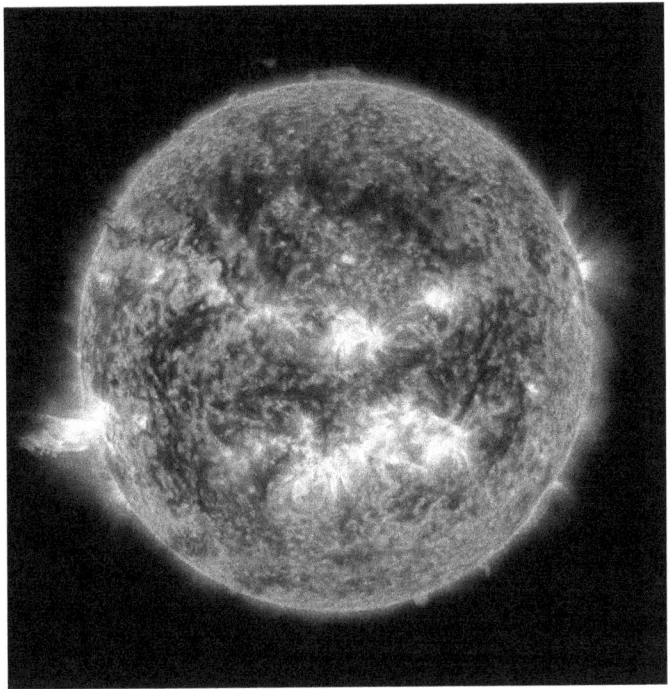

The sun plays a pivotal role in horary astrology.
https://www.flickr.com/photos/gsfc/9103296900

The Sun is one of the most important planets in a chart in horary astrology. It represents the querent, their soul journey, and their power or authority. The Sun can represent achievement, success, and recognition, which often positively influences a question regarding those aspects. Symbolically, it indicates wealth, honor, and fame due to hard work and dedication. The sun's impact in horary astrology signifies luck or favorability for querent's actions.

Meaning and Interpretation of the Sun in Horary Astrology

The Sun is interpreted as a signifier of leadership qualities and self-assertiveness. It can indicate taking control of your life and making decisions independently or with confidence. The Sun in a chart can mean energy is abundant, so new projects undertaken by the querent could succeed with effort. Whether taking on a business venture or starting something personal, like building a family home, the Sun is important in giving hope for success in these pursuits.

The sign under which the Sun falls will show how best to take advantage of its power during a situation. For instance, if the Sun is in Aries, it might symbolize entering into bold actions with an assurance that luck will favor them regardless of the obstacles. In contrast, if the Sun is in Capricorn, it could suggest working hard toward achieving goals with meticulous planning and persistence, but within realistic limits.

Overall, through horary astrology, the Sun gives an understanding of how a person should approach life's challenges with optimism while staying mindful.

Moon

The moon represents changing moods and the concept of stability in horary.
https://www.pexels.com/photo/photo-of-moon-47367/

The Moon is associated with the ocean, emotions, feelings, and femininity. It is a symbol of fluidity, transformation, and movement. In horary astrology, it represents changing moods and reassurance or stability. It reflects a person's inner world, hidden thoughts and desires, and past influences and patterns still affecting the present. The Moon has been connected to many goddesses, such as Hecate, Diana, and Artemis, who symbolize fertility, growth, and abundance. The Moon is closely tied to motherly love, empathy, and intuition. It moves quickly between the points of its orbit while reflecting light from the Sun onto the Earth.

Meaning and Interpretation of the Moon in Horary Astrology

The Moon is a significator for the querent's feelings, thoughts, desires, and emotions. It reflects how a person feels at the present moment and acts as an indicator of future events. The Moon can signify a person's moods, attitude toward life, and level of contentment. Horary astrology can represent relationships, changes, or transitions that will occur soon. Depending on its placement in the chart, it might point to financial gain or loss. Furthermore, when considering a relationship (business or romantic), both parties are represented by two different Moons depending on which house they occupy.

The South Node in Horary Astrology

The South Node of the Moon signifies the querent's past influences and patterns. It reflects how they felt in the past, including their childhood experiences and family relationships. The South Node can indicate things holding them back, like outdated beliefs or habits no longer serving them, and it points to people from the past. When interpreting the South Node in horary astrology, looking at its placement in relation to other planets and determining which areas of life it affects is critical.

The North Node in Horary Astrology

The North Node of the Moon represents the querent's current direction, goals, and desires. It points to the areas of life where a person is growing and evolving. The North Node is a guiding light, showing the querent's true potential and what they can achieve. This node reflects the querent's relationship with their higher self, including spiritual guidance or insight through interpreting it in a horary chart.

The Moon is significant in horary astrology as it indicates someone's feelings, emotions, and thoughts. It relates to changes occurring within a person and their relationships and transitions soon taking place in life.

Mercury

Mercury in horary astrology is crucial since it is associated with communication, commerce, and travel. The meaning and purpose of Mercury in horary astrology is to understand how a person's thoughts, words, and actions will be affected by their environment.

Mercury is the messenger of the gods.
https://pixabay.com/es/illustrations/mercurio-planeta-espacio-universo-5556108/

Meaning and Interpretation of Mercury in Horary Astrology

In horary astrology, Mercury is known as the Messenger of the gods. It symbolizes intellect, reason, wit, understanding, and creativity. Its main purpose is to provide insight into a person's mental state to manage emotions and behavior better. It helps develop self-awareness to make sound decisions based on the best interests rather than impulse or emotion.

Mercury's meaning and interpretation in horary astrology go beyond communication-related matters. It brings change and transformation through its symbolism of ideas and movement. This planet drives ambition and can help individuals overcome obstacles or start new projects. It teaches thinking outside the box and encourages exploring different perspectives of a situation or problem. Furthermore, its influence encourages people to take action, helping them to act on their ideas quickly instead of waiting too long or getting caught up in analysis paralysis.

Venus

Venus represents the feminine principle and can offer insight into the core needs of relationships. Venus represents beauty, harmony, love, money, friendship, and partnerships. The placement of Venus in a chart can reveal a lot about an individual's preferences and overall attitude.

Venus represents values and desires.
https://pixabay.com/es/illustrations/venus-planeta-espacio-universo-5556107/

Meaning and Interpretation of Venus in Horary Astrology

Venus indicates the querent's values and desires and how they seek them out in horary astrology. It shows the curiosities they possess, making them unique. Moreover, it indicates relationships they will likely attract or become involved in. Are they fleeting or long-term? Do they bring joy or sorrow?

Venus symbolizes creativity, gracefulness, balance, and abundance. It stands for fertility in its traditional sense (giving birth) and less literal sense (creating art). Therefore, Venus's appearance in a chart suggests potential success and reward through creative expression or ventures.

The interpretation of Venus in horary astrology depends on what part of its symbolism resonates with the querent's life at the moment. Suppose another point in the chart indicates a lack of harmony or interpersonal conflict. In that case, it suggests the querent should cultivate more balance in their relationships. It could be through strengthening the bonds with others similarly interested in harmony and peacekeeping efforts. On the other hand, if money is an issue, then Venus could indicate that now might be a good time to take action toward earning additional income or making investments with steady returns over time.

Mars

Mars is often called the "Lesser Malefic" in horary astrology. It symbolizes action, energy, and assertiveness. Its aspects can directly bring results and can often create accidents or spur quarrels and injuries. Due to its fiery nature, it is a powerful force of transformation, pushing the querent forward toward their goals yet creating obstacles along the way. Mars symbolizes physical effort, courage, ambition, and taking risks to succeed. It encourages people to face their fears while maintaining determination and focusing on the desired outcome.

Mars represents strength and passion.
https://pixabay.com/es/illustrations/marte-espacio-planeta-planetas-7723123/

Meaning and Interpretation of Mars in Horary Astrology

Mars is associated with masculine energy and embodies strength, power, passion, and aggression, positively or negatively. For example, regarding love, if someone is looking for a new romantic partner, they must have the courage to make themselves visible; otherwise, nothing will happen. Mars represents this part of people that helps them overcome inhibitions or doubts so they can confidently move forward.

It is necessary to recognize that the planet is about taking decisive action using willpower and perseverance to reach objectives and understand Mars's horary purpose. It enables a person to break through difficulties but warns against being reckless or careless since it has a destructive side, which could lead to dangerous consequences. Ultimately it teaches how channeling energy into productive means can help bring forth positive outcomes, even in difficult situations!

Jupiter

In horary astrology, Jupiter is called the *Greater Benefic* and represents luck, opportunity, growth, long journeys, higher education, and prophecy. Jupiter reflects querent's ambitions, wishes, and desires and relates to long-term prospects or opportunities likely to benefit them. In horary astrology, it can indicate the outcome of an event or situation or give insight into a possible future development.

Jupiter represents wealth and success.
https://pixabay.com/es/photos/j%c3%bapiter-plancta-espacio-6938302/

Meaning and Interpretation of Jupiter in Horary Astrology

The symbolism associated with Jupiter includes material wealth (including money) and success through hard work. In horary astrology, Jupiter denotes honor, respect, and prosperity. It represents truthfulness and justice but can be excessive when too strong or unbalanced due to unfavorable aspects from other planets.

Jupiter is associated with optimism and hope in horary astrology. It can indicate potential good fortune and abundance or a period of good luck. However, it can represent bad judgment, leading to overindulgence and wastefulness if not managed properly. Aspects of Jupiter can suggest the need for individuals to take risks or become more adventurous to achieve their goals.

Jupiter's influence on a chart provides insight into how an individual can approach life's opportunities and challenges. Its placement indicates their luck and ability to make wise decisions with difficult choices. A strong Jupiter position suggests that an individual will likely be blessed with luck, whereas a weak placement could indicate being more cautious to reap the rewards.

Overall, Jupiter represents the ability of individuals to recognize and use good fortune when presented. It encourages taking risks and trusting that decisions will lead to prosperity. Understanding its symbolism, meaning, and interpretation can help align people's actions with potential success.

Saturn

Saturn is the greater malefic in horary astrology and has a powerful influence over the chart. It rules burdens, karmic lessons, ambitions, debts, delays, poverty, obstacles, and death. Traditional texts associated it with fathers, old people, and various restrictions. It symbolizes hard work, discipline, and perseverance in pursuit of goals. When Saturn is prominent in a chart, it can indicate struggles and difficulties that must be overcome before real progress can be made.

Saturn represents ambition and dedication.
https://pixabay.com/es/illustrations/saturno-planeta-espacio-universo-5550180/

Meaning and Interpretation of Saturn in Horary Astrology

Saturn symbolizes heavy burdens that must be met through dedication and hard work in horary astrology. It symbolizes ambition and dedication to long-term projects or goals. As the Greater Malefic, it represents setbacks or hardships to achieving ambitions. However difficult these times might be, they can teach valuable lessons if individuals embrace them with courage and resilience. Saturn reflects the capacity for delayed gratification, an important quality when planning projects or working toward long-term goals.

The interpretation of Saturn in a chart depends on its dignity (exaltation or detriment) and whether angular, cadent, or intercepted within the chart wheel. Saturn indicates obstacles that must be overcome, but this will depend on other aspects within the chart. If other planets are helping bring success, then these challenges will not seem so daunting and will eventually lead to success. If no aspects from other planets indicate success, then these difficulties could become more serious over time, leading to delays or even failure.

When Saturn is well placed within a chart, it can indicate good things coming from hard work or effort put into long-term projects, like building a business or raising a family. Despite setbacks, these long-term investments will eventually lead to great rewards if the individual stays focused on their goal throughout the challenges encountered on this journey. If Saturn is poorly placed, it can suggest obstacles or hardships might hinder efforts, leading to delays or complete failure. Caution should be exercised when embarking upon new ventures unless they have strong indications from other planets that success will ensue despite adversity. Finally, when interpreting Saturn, remember "no pain, no gain." Often-encountered obstacles teach many valuable lessons if people confront them with courage and resilience.

Uranus

Uranus's position holds great significance in horary astrology, symbolizing a wide range of meanings and interpretations when in various houses or aspects. For a deeper understanding, delving into Uranus's complex and multifaceted nature and how it affects the horary chart as a whole is essential.

Uranus represents revolution.
https://pixabay.com/es/illustrations/urano-planeta-espacio-5559037/

Uranus, the seventh planet from the Sun, holds a unique position in astrology as it is renowned for its association with sudden changes, revolution, and upheaval. Known as the planet of awakening, Uranus symbolizes the emergence of new ideas, inventive thinking, and breaking free from established norms. Its influence is evident in technology, science, and societal revolution realms. Uranus represents the urge for individual freedom, intellectual independence, and breaking the shackles of tradition and conventionality.

Meaning and Interpretation of Uranus in Horary Astrology

In horary astrology, the position of Uranus becomes especially significant when deciphering a horary chart or having a snapshot of the heavens at the specific moment when the astrologer studies the querent's question. The chart is analyzed to obtain answers and insights into the individual's doubts and queries about their life.

Depending on the house in which Uranus resides in the horary chart, the planet's influence could have various implications for the querent. For instance, in the first house, Uranus indicates that the querent is experiencing a radical change in their personality or identity. On the other hand, if found in the sixth house, Uranus could suggest an unexpected shift in the person's work or health conditions.

Additionally, the aspects Uranus forms with other planets in the horary chart can further intensify or mitigate its influence. For example, a harmonious aspect between Uranus and Venus may symbolize sudden positive relationship changes or creativity. A challenging aspect between Uranus and Saturn could imply resistance to change or a clash between the old and the new.

One of the fascinating dimensions of Uranus in horary astrology is its link to unpredictability and surprises. The energy of Uranus brings a hint of chaos, prompting the querent to embrace change and adapt to new, unexpected circumstances. The presence of Uranus in a horary chart suggests that standard methods of inquiry and established thought patterns may not be sufficient to resolve the issue. Alternatively, it could hint at a ground-breaking solution or innovative approach the querent has not yet considered.

Furthermore, Uranus is known to have a strong connection with groups, social organizations, and humanitarian causes. Therefore, its position in a horary chart could shed light on the querent's relationship with their community, participation in social activism, or collaboration with like-minded individuals.

Neptune

Existing at the furthest reaches of the solar system, Neptune is revered as the supreme ruler of dreams, intuition, imagination, art, and spiritual enlightenment. It represents mysterious forces and the elusive realm of the subconscious, often leading to profound insights and hidden truths. In this context, the meaning and interpretation of Neptune in horary astrology elucidate its notable impact on the outcome of inquiries and the lives of individuals.

Neptune represents spiritual wisdom and creative abilities.
https://pixabay.com/es/photos/neptuno-planeta-sistema-solar-67537/

Meaning and Interpretation of Neptune in Horary Astrology

Neptune can be an enriching and challenging presence in an astrological chart, depending on its placement and the aspects it forms with other planets. When Neptune occupies a prominent position, it bestows individuals with heightened intuition, creative abilities, and spiritual wisdom. These people are often deeply connected with mysticism and the arts and are considered artistically and spiritually gifted. So, Neptune stands out as a powerful force for inspiration, artistic expression, and spiritual enlightenment.

However, Neptune has the potential to challenge and bewilder, as its placement in a chart may indicate deception, confusion, or illusion. Negatively, it can lead an individual to experience uncertainty and disorientation in dealing with reality. It may manifest as fantasies, delusions, or even escapism in its bearer. The ethereal nature of Neptune signifies a vulnerability to addictive behavior, substance abuse, and other ungrounded pursuits.

For instance, inquiring about a querent's future in a horary chart, if Neptune is positioned in the Third House, which symbolizes communication, intellect, and the immediate environment, it could imply a period of confusion, misunderstandings, or false information. On the other hand, this placement may grant them exceptional creative thinking or a surge of inspiration in their intellectual and communicative endeavors.

The interpretation of Neptune in a horary chart depends on the question and the sign and house it occupies. For example, if a querent asks about their romantic prospects and Neptune is present in the Seventh House, representing partnerships, it could suggest their future relationships may be filled with illusions, dreams, and idealization. Understanding the varied aspects of Neptune in a horary chart ultimately allows the astrologer to discern the role Neptune plays, shaping the reading and guiding the individual accordingly.

Pluto

Pluto represents transformation, power, renewal, and deep, hidden secrets in horary astrology. As a ruling planet in horary charts, Pluto is a harbinger of profound revelations or radical changes that may take place in the native's life, depending on its position and aspects with other planetary bodies. As the furthest-known celestial body in the solar system, Pluto's influence is considered mysterious and enigmatic, often revealing truths lying beneath the surface or shedding light on the darker aspects of an individual's subconscious.

Pluto represents transformation.
https://pixabay.com/es/photos/plut%c3%b3n-planeta-espacio-astronom%c3%ada-6595130/

Meaning and Interpretation of Pluto in Horary Astrology

Pluto's placement in horary astrology adds a significant layer of depth and meaning to a horary question. Interpreting a horary chart, an astrologer will scrutinize Pluto's location within the zodiac sign, house, and the aspects with other planets to unveil its potential influence on the querent's life circumstances.

When Pluto is prominently featured in a horary chart, it might indicate the question requires truth-seeking, transformation, or confronting and overcoming something deeply buried within the querent. Essentially, Pluto's presence in the astrological chart points toward a deep-seated issue or challenge the individual must confront and surmount to embark on a new path toward spiritual growth and personal evolution.

For instance, if Pluto is situated in the third house of the horary chart, which corresponds to communication, intellectual pursuits, and the local environment, an astrologer may deduce that the question involves a significant change or challenges related to these areas. The querent may be in a situation where they must express their thoughts or engage in difficult conversations to bring about the necessary transformations.

The aspects formed by Pluto in a horary chart shed light on the potential outcomes and challenges faced by the querent. Notably, Pluto's aspects with powerful planets like Saturn can suggest the person may have to navigate through obstacles or restrictions to reach their desired goal.

Similarly, a harmonious aspect between Pluto and Venus might hint that a transformative experience in the realms of love, relationships, or personal values could profoundly impact the querent's life. On the other hand, if Pluto has challenging aspects, it could indicate potential disruptions, upheavals, or events that test the individual's strength and resilience.

Chapter 6: Planetary Dignities and Joys

Have you heard of horary astrology and wondered what it is all about? One of the initial steps in understanding horary charts is comprehending the concept of the dignities and joys of planets. This critical concept recognizes the power, authority, or dignity of a planet to the chart being studied. When applying this principle, the analysis focuses on the traditional rulership qualities associated with each planet, deciphering Ptolemy's chart and calculating the same signs of dignity or strength that exist. This magnification of each planet's ability allows an astrologer to gauge an individual's joys and their respective growth position within the chart. This analysis can suggest areas where an individual succeeds or struggles, giving insight into their true potential for success. Understanding the planet's dignities and joys can be one of the most complex aspects of horary astrology - but it can prove highly rewarding for those pursuing this path.

What Are Dignities?

In horary astrology, dignities refer to the specific positions of a celestial body in the sky. In particular, they determine how well a planet is placed in a sign. Dignities factor into many aspects of horary astrology, like the strength of an individual's character or destiny and their place in the world. The term "dignity" comes from the Latin *dignus*, meaning "possessing worth."

There are five traditional dignities in horary astrology: domicile (the sign a planet is most powerful in), exaltation (the sign where it is second-most strong), detriment (the weakest position for a planet), fall (the second weakest), and triplicity (to do with elements). Knowing each planet's dignities is important because it helps create a clear picture of how each function within the chart and their influence on the outcome. For example, suppose a planet is in its domicile or exaltation. In that case, it will be stronger than in its detriment or fall.

Knowing these dignities allows for interpreting different planetary combinations more accurately. For example, when two planets are conjunct in a chart, you can determine which is more likely to take precedence by looking at their respective dignities. If one has strong dignity and the other weak, the stronger one will likely dominate the weaker one. It helps distinguish between positive and negative outcomes for certain questions or situations.

What Are Joys?

The term "joys" in astrology refers to the specific houses associated with each of the seven traditional planets. Each planet is assigned to a particular house. A planet is said to be "rejoicing" when it is in its "joys," as explained below.

In other words, the planet is at its strongest influence when placed in the corresponding house.

Knowing the planet's joys in horary astrology can be helpful because they provide insight into how different planetary energies manifest within a chart. For example, if Jupiter were placed in the 11th house, luck and good fortune would likely come your way, as Jupiter's joy lies in this house. Conversely, Saturn would bring feelings of restriction or limitation if placed in its joy (the 12th house). Therefore, understanding the joys allows an astrologer to quickly identify which energies will likely be dominant at any given time and interpret their influence on an individual's life.

The Joys of Planets

Planet	Joys
Sun	9th House
Moon	3rd House
Mercury	1st House
Venus	5th House
Mars	6th House
Jupiter	11th House
Saturn	12th House

Ptolemy's Chart on Essential Dignities

Ptolemy, a renowned astronomer, mathematician, and astrologer in the 2nd century CE, developed a chart illustrating the dignities and rulership of the celestial bodies. This chart represents the complex dynamics and correspondences between the planets, zodiac signs, and astrology houses, enabling astrologers to make sense of the myriad influences in the cosmos.

A Table of the Essential Dignities of the PLANETS according to Ptolemy

Sign	Houses of the Planets	Exaltation	Triplicity of Planets		The Terms of the Planets					The Faces of the Planets			Detriment	Fall
			D	N										
♈	♂ D	☉ 19	☉	♃	♃ 6	♀ 14	☿ 21	♂ 26	♄ 30	♂ 10	☉ 20	♀ 30	♀	♄
♉	♀ N	☽ 3	♀	☽	♀ 8	☿ 15	♃ 22	♄ 26	♂ 30	☿ 10	☽ 20	♄ 30	♂	
♊	☿ D	☊ 3	♄	☿	☿ 7	♃ 14	♀ 21	♄ 25	♂ 30	♃ 10	♂ 20	☉ 30	♃	
♋	☽ D/N	♃ 15	♂	♂	♂ 6	♃ 13	☿ 20	♀ 27	♄ 30	♀ 10	☿ 20	☽ 30	♄	♂
♌	☉ D/N		☉	♃	♄ 6	☿ 13	♀ 19	♃ 25	♂ 30	♄ 10	♃ 20	♂ 30	♄	
♍	☿ N	☿ 15	♀	☽	☿ 7	♀ 13	♃ 18	♄ 24	♂ 30	☉ 10	♀ 20	☿ 30	♃	♀
♎	♀ D	♄ 21	♄	☿	♄ 6	♀ 11	♃ 19	☿ 24	♂ 30	☽ 10	♄ 20	♃ 30	♂	☉
♏	♂ N		♂	♂	♂ 6	♃ 14	♀ 21	☿ 27	♄ 30	♂ 10	☉ 20	♀ 30	♀	☽
♐	♃ D	☋ 3	☉	♃	♃ 8	♀ 14	☿ 19	♄ 25	♂ 30	☿ 10	☽ 20	♄ 30	☿	
♑	♄ N	♂ 28	♀	☽	♀ 6	☿ 12	♃ 19	♂ 25	♄ 30	♃ 10	♂ 20	☉ 30	☽	♃
♒	♄ D		♄	☿	♄ 6	☿ 12	♀ 20	♃ 25	♂ 30	♀ 10	☿ 20	☽ 30	☉	
♓	♃ N	♀ 27	♂	♂	♀ 8	♃ 14	☿ 20	♂ 26	♄ 30	♄ 10	♃ 20	♂ 30	☿	☿

The rows in Ptolemy's Chart of Dignities display a comprehensive understanding of each planet's roles and influences over the zodiac signs. This chart is based on the ancient astrological system of dignities and debilities. It presents a hierarchical order of planetary influences on each zodiac sign, determining their strength, weakness, or level of affinity with other celestial bodies.

The first column of Ptolemy's Chart of Dignities enumerates the twelve zodiac signs, starting with Aries and ending with Pisces. Each sign has unique characteristics, qualities, and symbolic meanings that directly influence the lives and personalities of those born under them.

The second column of the chart, known as the rulers of the signs, lists the traditional planetary rulers associated with each zodiac sign. These rulers are considered the planets with natural "houses" or "homes" within the signs they rule. For example, Mars rules Aries and Scorpio, making these signs its natural domain. A planet within its own sign has a strong influence, resulting in its qualities flourishing.

The third column reveals where each planet is considered exalted and the specific degree of exaltation. Exaltation is a powerful and fortunate position for a planet, signifying its highest potential of expression and influence within the sign, often bringing prosperity and success. For instance, the Sun is exalted in Aries at the 19th degree. This degree is particularly potent, but generally, the entire sign confers a heightened dignity to the exalted planet.

The planetary rulership of triplicities - the groups of three signs sharing the same basic nature – fire, earth, air, and water- are represented in the fourth column. Here, you can observe how the fire triplicity of Aries, Leo, and Sagittarius repeats itself. Each triplicity ruler bestows its elemental qualities on the corresponding signs, further empowering and shaping them.

The fifth column unveils the specific degrees where rulership by term, known as bound rulership, occurs. This scheme divides each sign into five unequal segments, with each planet ruling a specific degree range. For example, Jupiter rules the first six degrees of Aries, signifying that Jupiter has some influence within this degree range.

The sixth column of Ptolemy's chart represents the rulership by face, known as decanates. It breaks down each zodiac sign into three distinct 10-degree segments, each ruled by a specific planet. For instance, in Aries, Mars rules the first 10 degrees (0°00' - 9°59'), the Sun rules the next 10 degrees (10°00' - 19°59'), and a different planet governs the third 10 degrees. This adds depth to understanding how planets influence zodiac signs within specific degree ranges. It helps astrologers interpret specific degrees in a chart, providing a more detailed analysis of an individual's planetary placements.

The seventh column focuses on the detriment concept, occurring when a planet is in a sign opposite the one it rules. This placement is considered unfavorable because the planet is at a disadvantage, far from its natural home. Consequently, the characteristics associated with the planet are often weakened or obstructed. Each planet in Ptolemy's chart, except for the Sun and Moon, has two signs of detriment, one to the opposite of each of its two ruling signs.

The eighth column describes a planet's fall, a situation where a planet is located opposite to the sign of its exaltation. When a planet is in exaltation, it is at its highest period of expression and power. It is in a weakened state when it is in the opposing sign or fall. In these scenarios, the positive qualities of the planet are diminished, and astrologers could interpret it as a challenging or unfavorable influence in a chart. Like the concept of exaltation, each planet has only one sign for exaltation and fall.

Planets and Their Dignities and Joy

Sun

The Sun's dignities and joys, as derived from Ptolemy's chart, hold significant importance in understanding the influence of celestial bodies on our personalities and lives in astrology. The chart meticulously analyzes the Sun's influence in various astrological signs and houses, indicating specific qualities it possesses and the respective strengths in different placements. Exploring each facet of these complex concepts is crucial to deeply grasping what the Sun's dignities and joys convey.

The Sun's dignities reflect its inherent power, prestige, and influence in different astrological signs. It refers to the relationship between the Sun and certain signs enhancing or diminishing its potency. There are four hierarchical levels of dignities: domiciles or rulership, exaltation, triplicity, and term or bounds. Each level signifies a particular degree of authority the Sun possesses in different placements.

The Sun is the dominant and natural ruler of the zodiac sign of Leo. It asserts a direct and tremendous influence on the qualities of this fiery sign. Leos, in turn, are governed by energizing, warm, and confident characteristics associated with the Sun.

Aries is the exaltation sign for the Sun, considered in its highest potency. In this placement, the Sun demonstrates a powerful and jubilant expression of its traits, rendering Aries individuals determined, enthusiastic, and charismatic.

The Sun rules the fire triplicity, including Aries, Leo, and Sagittarius. Consequently, individuals born under these signs exhibit pronounced characteristics of ambition, passion, and self-motivation that the Sun embodies.

In Ptolemy's chart, there are specific degrees within astrological signs wherein the Sun is considered to have mild authority. Although not remarkably influential, these placements reflect minute control over the person's characteristics and life events.

In addition to dignities, the Sun's joy is in a specific house of the astrological chart – the 9th House. This house represents philosophy, religion, higher education, foreign travel, and broader perceptions. Since the Sun is universally acknowledged as the celestial symbol of vitality, consciousness, and self-expression, its association with the 9th house reflects the joy of expanding intellectual horizons, discovering new experiences, and seeking the truth.

Moon

The Moon, one of the seven classical planets in traditional astrology, has its dignities and joy giving deeper insights into its impact on an individual's life.

In the Ptolemy chart, the Moon's dignities are categorized into different levels; essential and accidental. Essential dignity refers to the positions where the Moon can express itself most powerfully without being hindered by other astrological factors. These positions are known as Rulership, where a planet is considered most at home to express itself most effectively. For the Moon, this position is in the zodiac sign of Cancer, where it is the natural ruler. The Moon can fully express its nurturing, intuitive, and emotional side, bringing strong comfort, security, and sensitivity to the individual's life.

In the Ptolemy chart, the Moon is exalted in the sign of Taurus, allowing the individual to tap into its supportive, grounding, and productive qualities. With the Moon in this position, people can use its steady, dependable energy to lay the grounds for solid relationships and living foundations.

On the other hand, accidental dignity refers to the contextual factors helping improve the Moon's influence, like its placement in specific houses within a person's birth chart. A planet's Joy indicates the position where it performs best, and for the Moon, this is the third house of communication, siblings, and the local environment. This association with the third house is interesting, as the third house corresponds to a person's life strategy and highlights the Moon's connection with the emotional aspects of communication and relationships with the local community.

Mercury

In Ptolemy's chart, the essential dignities of Mercury are highlighted to showcase the planetary characteristics and strengths, depending on the various positions within the zodiac signs. Ptolemy's chart reveals the detailed dignities and the joy of Mercury to understand its overall astrological significance better. Mercury's essential dignities are classified into five categories: domicile, exaltation, triplicity, term, and face (or decan).

Mercury's domicile is in the mutable air signs of Gemini and Virgo. Mercury displays its full potential when residing in these zodiac signs enabling individuals to manifest better communication skills, curiosity, adaptability, and analytical thinking. Mercury is at ease in its domicile, and people with this placement can effectively utilize its energies.

Mercury is exalted in the sign of Virgo, meaning Mercury has an especially powerful expression in Virgo than in other positions. In Virgo, Mercury enjoys the benefits of its domicile and gets an extra boost in strength. It enhances intellectual abilities, better use of logical reasoning, and a more practical and organized approach to life.

The term "triplicity" describes the classical division of the twelve zodiac signs into three groups of the four elements of fire, earth, air, and water. This classification considers Mercury, the ruler of the air triplicity, including the air signs of Gemini, Libra, and Aquarius. Mercury's communicative, social, and intellectual traits are emphasized in these signs. They manifest as the ability to adapt to various social settings swiftly, driving individuals with this placement to become more influential in their environment.

As per Ptolemy's chart, Mercury has rulership in specific terms across all twelve signs, allowing enhanced expression of its energies during certain degrees of each sign. Depending on their birth chart, these specific degrees can modify how Mercury's influence is felt individually.

Next is Face or Decan. The signs are divided into three decans or faces, each consisting of 10 degrees. Mercury is the ruler of the first decan of Gemini and Virgo to heighten its influence and abilities in these signs. Those born with Mercury in these decans could find stronger analytical, perceptive, and communicative talents, resulting in more significant expression of Mercury's energies in their lives.

Mercury joy is in the first house – a position known as the "helm" or "ascendant." Mercury's residence in the first house reinforces personal identity and expression, allowing individuals to adeptly demonstrate their intellectual and communicative abilities. Those with Mercury in the first house can have a natural ease when interacting with others, exchanging ideas, and asserting their perspective.

Venus

Venus's dignities are primarily based on the planet's position within specific zodiac signs, ruling over two signs: Taurus and Libra. Venus is considered in its domicile when placed in these signs, meaning its natural characteristics are enhanced and strengthened. In Taurus, Venus influences sensual and material desires, cultivating a love of beauty, comfort, and stability. In Libra, Venus's signature focuses more on partnership, balance, and fairness, encouraging diplomacy and harmonious relationships.

Besides its domicile, Venus has a significant relationship with another astrological configuration: exaltation. It occurs when Venus is in Pisces, elevating its natural characteristics to their highest potential. In this placement, the planet's energies reflect an unconditional, spiritual love and compassion, transcending the material realm and fostering deeper empathy and understanding.

Conversely, Venus experiences detriment when positioned in Mars-ruled signs, Aries and Scorpio. In these placements, the planet's natural disposition is weakened, resulting in a more challenging expression of love, beauty, and harmony. Individuals with Venus in Aries or Scorpio might find it harder to express tenderness and placidity, leading to potential tensions in relationships, emotional volatility, or problems with self-worth.

Furthermore, Venus experiences its fall in Virgo, revealing the planet's weakest expression. In this meticulous earth sign, Virgo's analytical and critical nature dampens Venus's natural affinity for love, beauty, and harmony. As a result, individuals with Venus in Virgo might struggle to accept and express love in its purest form, often becoming overly critical of themselves and others.

Beyond dignities, Ptolemy's astrology describes the concept of Venus's joy, which occurs when Venus is placed in the fifth house of the birth chart. Here, Venus's association with love, beauty, creativity, and pleasure is allowed to fully manifest and flourish, leading to a natural inclination toward artistic expression, romantic relationships, and personal enjoyment. This placement is considered auspicious, as Venus's energies align harmoniously with the fifth house's emphasis on self-expression and joyful experiences.

Mars

According to Ptolemy's chart, Mars, known as the red planet and the fourth planet from the Sun, holds significant astrological importance. Mars has particular dignities, which determine its power and effectiveness in the astrological chart. The primary dignity of Mars is its rulership and exaltation in the signs of Aries, Scorpio, and Capricorn. Mars is most potent and influential when it is in Aries or Scorpio, while Mars in Capricorn is at its peak effectiveness. In these positions, Mars expresses its natural qualities of assertiveness, courage, aggression, and competitiveness with greater ease, positively impacting individuals born under these signs.

On the other hand, Mars has its detriments and falls in the signs of Libra and Cancer. Mars is considered weaker and less effective during these placements, as its natural attributes are challenged, negatively impacting individuals born under these signs or with less intensity.

The concept of *joys* refers to the special connection between certain planets and specific houses in the horoscope, according to Ptolemy's chart. Mars is associated with the joy in the 6th House, primarily linked to work, service, health, and daily routines. Mars' connection to this house signifies a proactive approach, discipline, and strategic thinking when dealing with work and health matters. It can indicate a strong sense of duty and responsibility in these areas.

In symbolic terms, Mars' dignities and joys in Ptolemy's chart depict the energy and influence it has on individuals in different positions in the zodiac. Mars governs drive, determination, assertiveness, and passion, making it a decisive force in defining an individual's mannerisms, motivations, and ambitions, especially during interactions with work, service, and health.

Jupiter

Jupiter's dignities and joy in Ptolemy's Chart provide a detailed understanding of the planet's astrological significance, its influence on human life, and the various areas it governs.

Jupiter, often called the *king of the gods* in Roman mythology, is the largest planet in the solar system and represents abundance, growth, and optimism in astrology. Its dignities in Ptolemy's Chart are closely tied to the zodiac signs it rules and its various relationships. The dignities give different levels of power to the planet based on the zodiac sign it is in. Jupiter's major dignities are as follows:

Jupiter rules over the signs of Sagittarius and Pisces. When it is in these signs, it is in its domicile, and its positive qualities are displayed most effectively in individuals born under these signs. Individuals with a strong Jupiter influence could exhibit benevolence, generosity, wisdom, and a strong desire to pursue knowledge.

Jupiter is exalted in the sign of Cancer, signifying that its beneficial influences are amplified when positioned in it. People with Jupiter in Cancer enjoy great emotional wealth, nurturing instincts, and an affinity for home and family life.

In triplicity in Ptolemy's chart, Jupiter governs the water signs – Cancer, Scorpio, and Pisces – indicating the planet's expression of natural affinity for those individuals born under these signs. As a result, their lives may be enhanced with heightened creativity, intuition, and emotional depth.

Ptolemy assigned specific degree ranges within each zodiac sign where a celestial body exhibits particular influence or affinity. Jupiter's "terms" are within portions of each zodiac sign where these traits are most operative.

The face dignity, known as decan, divides each zodiac sign into three equal segments of 10 degrees, ruled by three different planets. Jupiter rules specific faces in different signs, bestowing its nobility and good fortune to those born under these placements.

Regarding its joy, Jupiter is most favorably placed in the eleventh house of the astrological chart, defined as the house of good fortune or the house of friends. This placement emphasizes the auspiciousness associated with friendships, aspirations, and achievements. In the 11th house, Jupiter's ability to bring about growth, expansion, and celebration is heightened, allowing individuals with this position to benefit from strong social networks, philanthropy, and long-term goals realizations.

Understanding Jupiter's dignities and joy in Ptolemy's Chart provides crucial insights into the planet's astrological significance and influence on human life. It sheds light on Jupiter's relationships with the zodiac signs and how its energy manifests in people's lives. As the planet is associated with abundance, growth, and optimism, Jupiter's dignities and placements reveal the path to good fortune and success in various spheres of life.

Saturn

Saturn is the planet of structure, responsibility, and authority in horary astrology. Saturn's energy reflects a deep sense of duty, commitment, and determination to complete tasks excellently. It can reflect a person's psychological state, security, and stability. Through Ptolemy's wheel chart in horary astrology, insight is gained into how Saturn's influence manifests in each sign.

Saturn, the 6th planet from the Sun, is prominent in astrology and Ptolemy's chart of dignities and joys. Ptolemy's chart reveals Saturn's various strengths and weaknesses, depending on its position in the zodiac and its relationship with other celestial bodies. Saturn's dignities include its sign of rulership, exaltation, and triplicity, which determine its level of power and influence over an individual's life and character.

In Ptolemy's chart, Saturn has its sign of rulership in Capricorn and Aquarius. Therefore, Saturn is the most potent and effective in these signs, leading to increased discipline, structure, and ambitions for people with Saturn strongly placed in Capricorn or Aquarius. Saturn's exaltation is in Libra, signifying its next most powerful position. Saturn brings balance, justice, and strong critical thinking skills when well-aspect in a natal chart.

Triplicity rulership is another aspect of dignity, shared among three planets for the four elements (fire, earth, air, and water). Saturn has triplicity rulership in the air signs - Gemini, Libra, and Aquarius - further emphasizing its affinity with intellectual pursuits and communication.

The joys refer to the specific connection between the traditional planets and the twelve houses in astrology. Saturn's joy is in the 12th house - the house of introspection and self-undoing. This placement allows Saturn's inherent wisdom and introspective nature to reflect upon past actions and facilitate spiritual growth.

Chapter 7: Major Planetary Aspects

One of astrology's most fascinating elements is its planetary aspects. It is the concept of the solar system's planets influencing the lives of humans through their movements and alignment. Understanding astrology requires learning about its five main planetary aspects: oppositions, trines, squares, sextiles, and conjunctions. Each aspect is significant when interpreting a person's horoscope. This chapter takes you on a journey through these aspects to uncover deeper astrology secrets.

Horary Charts and the Five Planetary Aspects

One of the biggest benefits of studying planetary aspects is they can help you make better life decisions. Understanding the planet's dynamics and interactions lets you know which decisions will likely lead to positive or negative results. You can use planetary aspects to predict the future to help determine how to proceed – and they also provide insight into relationships. Understanding how the planets influence each other and the energies they create, you get a better sense of how relationships will likely work out, improving communication with others and the dynamics of relationships. Studying planetary aspects offers a deeper understanding of yourself and your place in the universe. Learning the energies the planets create – and how they interact – provides a better understanding of individual energy and how it is used in harmony with the universe. It can be a powerful tool for personal growth and development.

Major aspects are the angles between the planets and describe their relationship. Usually formed when two planets are a certain number of degrees apart, this number of degrees is known as the "orb." Aspect patterns form when several planets are connected in a certain way, known as a "configuration," essential for understanding and interpreting the birth chart. Astrologers rely on this specific mix of planetary energies to interpret the planetary forces in the birth chart and analyze how they affect the native's life. Aspects have different meanings depending on which planets are involved and their position in the chart. The most basic aspects are:

- The Conjunction
- The Sextile
- The Square
- The Trine
- The Opposition

Each has a different meaning and influence on the planets. It determines the current positions of the planets in the sky and analyzes the aspects between them. For example:

- **A conjunction** occurs when two planets are in the same degree of the zodiac and is considered a very close relationship between them. This aspect indicates a deep union between two people or a powerful connection between two events.
- **A sextile** occurs when two planets are in the same sign but at a 60-degree angle from each other. This aspect indicates a strong connection between two people or a strong energy between two events
- **A square** occurs when two planets are in the same sign but at a 90-degree angle from each other. This aspect indicates a challenging relationship between two people or a struggle between two events
- **A trine** takes place when two planets are in the same sign but at a bigger angle from each other, or about 120 degrees. This aspect indicates a harmonious relationship between two people or an easy flow of energy between two events

- **An opposition** occurs when two planets are in the same sign but at a 180-degree angle from each other. This aspect indicates an intense relationship (similar to a square but less extreme) between two people or a struggle between two events.

Understanding these five planetary aspects is essential to interpret a birth chart and understanding the native's energies and influences. Let's explore each one further.

The Conjunction

Conjunctions are an interesting phenomenon, adding an extra layer of meaning to an answer. They are two or more planets together in close proximity in the zodiac. Essentially, they are the relationship between two planets or points in a horoscope, like the Ascendant, the Midheaven, or a particular house cusp. This relationship is established when the two planets or points are placed within a certain angular separation from each other, usually from 0° to 8°. The conjunction's orb creates an energetic connection between the planets with positive and negative effects. For instance, when two planets are in conjunction, they amplify each other's energy, creating a powerful effect.

On the other hand, if the planets are in opposition, they create tension and conflict. The effect's strength depends on the degree of the conjunction, the planets involved, and the sign where the conjunction takes place. The closer the two points are, the stronger the influence of the conjunction. For example, two planets *in the same sign or house indicate* a strong bond, like friendship or partnership. In contrast, two planets in *opposing signs* or houses mean a struggle or conflict between them.

The Conjunction refers to the energies of two planets combined. When two planets are in the same sign or house, the combined energies of the planets will be more powerful than the individual planet's energies. For example, suppose two planets are in the sign of Aries. In that case, the combined energy might be interpreted as strong, passionate, and courageous energy.

How Conjunction Work in the Charts

Conjunctions bring out the special relationship between the planets involved, amplifying their influence and intensifying their energies. Every conjunction has a specific energy. For example, the conjunction of:

- Jupiter and Saturn signify a period of great success and accomplishment
- Mars and Neptune bring out creativity and self-expression
- Mars and Venus in the chart indicate a passionate relationship
- Saturn and the Sun indicate a period of struggle and difficulty

Conjunctions can identify the planets' or points' impact on each other. For example, a conjunction between the Moon and Jupiter indicates the Moon is influencing Jupiter's energy. A conjunction between the Sun and Saturn indicates the Sun is suppressing Saturn's ability to bring about positive results.

Conjunctions provide insight into the relationship between planets and points in the chart. For example, a conjunction between Mercury and Jupiter indicates Mercury influencing Jupiter's ability to manifest its goals and ambitions, while one between the Moon and Mars indicates the Moon is affecting Mars' ability to achieve desired outcomes.

The Sextile

The Sextile is an aspect of astrology describing the relationship between two planets 60 degrees apart. It is considered a "soft" aspect, which is less intense than the conjunction, trine, or square aspects. This harmonious angle between two planets acts as a bridge connecting two energies together. Since a sextile is quite auspicious and an indication of good things to come, it symbolizes a "meeting of the minds" and the formation of a strong and lasting connection between two planets. It signifies balance and stability and often manifests as creative energy, productive partnerships, and successful collaborations. The Sextile aspect is considered a "lucky" aspect because it can open the door to possibilities. For example:

- It indicates where you can find success and the areas where the most progress can be made.
- It indicates where natural talents and abilities lie and can point people in the right direction.

The sextile aspect can be used to understand relationships with others. For example:

- It shows how to work together with partners, family members, and friends.

- It identifies potential conflicts between two people or situations.

The Sextile shows signs of growth and development to promote self-discovery and advancement in life goals. It can be benefit answering questions about achieving ambitions.

How Sextile Work in the Charts

Let's look at how the sextile aspect works with more prominent celestial bodies to understand better how it works with different planets.

- When the Moon and the Sun are sextile, it indicates a strong connection to emotions.
- When Mercury and Venus are sextile, it shows the ability to express yourselves more easily and take risks without fear of failure.
- When Mars and Jupiter are sextile, it indicates optimism and motivation.
- When Saturn and the Moon are sextile, self-awareness and groundedness indicate a time for self-reflection.

Overall, the sextile aspect is a powerful tool that can help connect to emotions and push toward growth. Understanding how the sextile aspect works with the different planets can be advantageous.

The Square

Astrology is a field filled with complex and intricate concepts. One concept is the square aspect. It's easy to feel overwhelmed trying to understand what it means. It's called a square because this angle is 90°, making it look like a square when viewed on a chart. The planets or points in the square aspect are in two different signs and are usually a source of tension in the chart because the two planets' energies are at odds with each other.

The square is a sign of inner conflict between two opposite energies, and it can manifest in different ways. For instance:

- It manifests as a fear of failure, an inability to make decisions, or a fear of rejection.
- It manifests signs of being stuck and unable to move forward.

Balancing the two sides of the chart during a reading can be difficult. The astrologer must find a way to bring the two sides of the chart together to deal with this tension. It is necessary because, despite the problematic features of the square, it is a source of potential growth and transformation.

How The Square Work in the Charts

It is often said that when the square is present in the horoscope, it indicates a person's ability to face challenges and change their life. When paired with the different planets, squares interact differently. For example:

- When the Moon is in square aspect to the Sun, it signifies inner turmoil and difficulty balancing the need for attention and time for oneself.
- Venus and Jupiter show confusion between material matters and spiritual matters.
- Saturn and Mercury indicate fear of the unknown and a lack of confidence in deciding.
- Mercury and Venus reflect difficulty communicating and expressing feelings.
- Mars and Jupiter represent a person pushing themselves too hard and unable to control their ambitions.

The Trine

Astrology uses the trine to analyze a person's character and potential. It is shaped like a triangle and formed when two planets in a birth chart are approximately 120 degrees apart. When two planets are aligned this way, they often create favorable energy. The trine aspect is often compared to the square. While the square represents difficulty and struggle, the trine shows the opposite; luck and ease. This aspect can determine if a relationship will likely succeed in the long run. Trines provide insight into:

- The individual's actions and reactions to different situations.
- The individual's strengths and weaknesses and how they can best use them to their advantage.
- How the individual can best use their energies to create positive and beneficial changes in their life.

One of the most powerful effects of the trine is its ability to unlock hidden potential, enabling success in various fields.

How The Trine Work in the Charts

The trine aspect works differently for each planet, creating different effects in the chart.

- When the Moon is involved in a trine aspect, it shows emotional sensitivity and intuition. It indicates someone is more empathetic and open to others. With a trine aspect between the Sun and Moon, a person is more likely to find success and fulfillment in their life.

- When Mercury is involved in a trine aspect, it facilitates the ability to think clearly and logically. It indicates someone is articulate and communicative. With a trine aspect between Mercury and Venus, a person is more likely to find success in relationships and social engagements.

- When Venus is involved in a trine aspect, it shows an increased ability to express love and compassion. With a trine aspect between Venus and Mars, a person is more likely to find success in their creative endeavors.

- When Mars is involved in a trine aspect, it shows someone energetic and assertive. With a trine aspect between Mars and Jupiter, a person is more likely to find success in their career and business ventures.

- When Saturn is involved in a trine aspect, it indicates someone responsible and focused. With a trine aspect between Saturn and the Moon, a person is more likely to find success and stability in their life.

The Opposition

The opposition is an important aspect in horary charts as it reveals the tension between two entities. For instance, it can measure the relationship between two people or predict the outcome of a specific event. It can analyze the motives of both parties in a situation. The opposition formation occurs when two planets are just a 180 degrees angle apart. It creates tension between them that can be interpreted to gain insight into the situation.

The opposition is considered a major planetary aspect because it reveals the tension between two entities. It indicates conflict but can also indicate a coming together of forces. For instance, it can reveal the current state of a relationship between two people or the expected outcome of a certain event. It is possible to use the opposition to discover the hidden motives of the parties in a situation.

The opposition is a powerful tool for gaining insight into the energies in a particular situation. It can help identify areas of conflict and potential collaboration. By analyzing the opposition, you better understand the forces influencing a situation, make informed decisions, and avoid potential pitfalls.

The opposition is an aspect of tension and conflict in astrology because when two planets oppose each other, they are in disagreement and clash energetically. It creates tension and difficulty in the areas of life represented by the planets. For example, if the Moon and Mars were in opposition, it could indicate difficulty in relationships and emotions. However, the opposition has a positive side, bringing balance and harmony to the areas of life it affects. The opposing planets represent two sides of the same coin and bring out the best and worst in each other, essentially showing how balance can be achieved by understanding both sides of a situation. Oppositions profoundly impact life, as they indicate how to interact with the people and situations people encounter. It can also:

- Provide insight into relationships, as it can show how to interact with others and how interactions affect lives.
- To understand strengths and weaknesses and how to use them advantageously.

How the Opposition Work in the Charts

Opposition works differently with each planet and represents a tension between two points of view. For example, the Moon is the most sensitive planet, and its opposition acts as a buffer against the powerful, dominating energy of the sun. Other examples include:

- The opposition between Mercury and Venus creates a dynamic between reason and feeling.
- The opposition between Mars and Jupiter highlights the tension between power and growth.
- The opposition of Saturn and the Sun creates a balance between the conscious and unconscious.
- The opposition of Uranus and Neptune highlights the tension

between the material and spiritual worlds.

Each opposition works differently, creating different tension levels and enabling an understanding of how these planets work together and affect life. Ultimately, the opposition between the planets creates a push and pull between two forces, enabling people to create balanced, healthy lives.

Depending on the planets involved, the opposition can bring positive and negative qualities during a reading. For example:

- When the Moon is in opposition to the sun, it can evoke sensitivity or insecurity.
- When Mercury is in opposition to Venus, it reveals differences in communication styles. Mercury is more analytical, and Venus is more emotive, so this opposition creates an imbalanced energy between the two.
- When Mars is in opposition to Jupiter, it induces a competitive spirit. Jupiter is the planet of luck and abundance, while Mars is the planet of action and drive. When these two planets are in opposition, they create a spirit of rivalry as they push each other to be more ambitious.
- When Saturn is in opposition to another planet, it can induce fear and caution. Saturn is a planet of restrictions and limitations, and when in opposition to another, it causes a person to be overly cautious or pessimistic.

One of the most important aspects of astrology is learning how the major planetary aspects work. These planetary aspects are the links between the planets in the solar system and the energies produced by them. Understanding these aspects gives a better understanding of the energies in people's lives and how they can affect circumstances and experiences.

Chapter 8: Minor Planetary Aspects

As a complex field of study, astrology uses different categories of planetary aspects to interpret the movements of the planets and stars and their effects on people. Astrology is divided into major and minor aspects; each provides extra insight into chart analysis. Major aspects explored in chapter 7 are the main planetary configurations for interpreting a birth chart, while minor aspects add flair to prediction. This chapter explores the minor aspects of astrology and how to use them to gain an even deeper insight into the answers you seek.

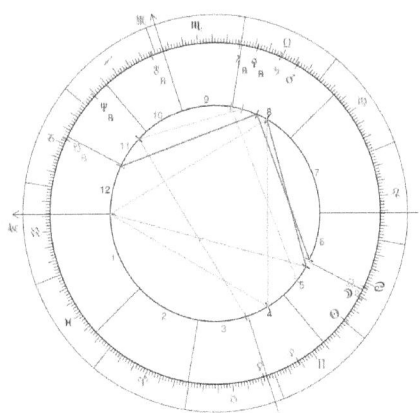

Planetary aspects on a birth chart.
Morn, CC BY-SA 3.0 <https://creativecommons.org/licenses/by-sa/3.0>, via Wikimedia Commons https://upload.wikimedia.org/wikipedia/commons/4/43/Natal_Chart_--_Adam.svg

Minor Astrological Aspects

Astrologers use various methods to interpret the positions of the stars, including using minor aspects. Minor aspects are the angular distances between planets less than 150 degrees, like 45 degrees, 60 degrees, and 72 degrees. They are less commonly used than the major aspects but are still vital to understanding the influence of the planets in a birth chart or reading. Astrologers use different minor aspects, but some of the most commonly used are sextiles, semi-squares, sesquiquadrates, quintiles, and quincunxes.

- The sextile is formed when two planets are 60 degrees apart and is often a harmonious aspect foreshadowing luck and opportunity.
- The semi-square is formed when two planets are 45 degrees apart and is a challenging aspect of predicting tension and conflict.
- The sesquiquadrate is formed when two planets are 135 degrees apart and is a difficult aspect showing stress and discord.
- The quintile is formed when two planets are 72 degrees apart and is an opportunity to create something new and unique.
- The quincunx is created when two planets are 150 degrees apart, and it represents complicated and surprising changes.

When astrologers use minor aspects, they look at the subtle influences between planets and how they influence different areas of life. For example:

- A minor aspect between Venus and Saturn indicates a person's relationship with authority.
- A minor aspect between the Sun and Mars indicates a person's ability to take action and be assertive.

Moreover, looking at the interconnections between planets, astrologists use minor aspects to determine how these planets affect an individual's life. For example:

- A minor aspect between Mars and the Sun indicates a person's drive and ambition.

- A minor aspect between Venus and Neptune indicates a person's ability to be creative and imaginative.

The minor aspects are often combined with other astrological techniques, such as transits, progressions, and midpoints, to form a more comprehensive understanding of how the planets influence someone. Overall, astrologers use minor aspects to look at the subtle connections between planets and gain insight into a person's character, strengths, and weaknesses. It helps them make more accurate readings and give better advice.

The Semi-Sextile

The semi-sextile planetary is created when two planets are apart by a 30-degree angle. It is an aspect of adjustment, meaning it helps people adjust to the energy of the planets involved and accept the changes they bring. For example:

- Encourages taking action and learning from mistakes.
- Draws connections between different areas of life.
- Compromises between two conflicting forces.

It is one of the so-called minor aspects of astrology, but it has a powerful influence on chart reading. During a reading, astrologers report the semi-sextile to:

- Signifies restlessness and dissatisfaction. It shows a sense of wanting more but not having the necessary motivation to take steps to get what they want. It is particularly helpful for those who feel stuck in a rut and unable to move forward.
- Predict uncertainty and confusion. It shows how someone questions their decisions and feels overwhelmed by their choices. It identifies someone with difficulty deciding and lacking confidence in their judgment.

Astrologers believe the energies associated with the semi-sextile can bring about positive and negative results.

- On the one hand, it inspires creativity and new ideas.
- On the other hand, it causes doubt and confusion.

These discrepancies occur because celestial energies are unique to each individual, depending on other aspects in their chart. Overall, the semi-sextile is an aspect that should not be overlooked. It can predict powerful and unique energies to unlock potential and provide insight into a person's personality and life path. However, its effects are limited. It cannot be used to signify drastic elements. Instead, it should be used to balance two conflicting forces.

How Semi-Sextile Work in the Charts

When the planets in a chart form a semi-sextile aspect, they can have a very subtle but powerful influence on a person's life. Essentially, they are in a state of tension and disagreement. They don't necessarily have to conflict with each other, but they can. This tension manifests in different ways, depending on the other aspects and positions in the horoscope. It has the potential to bring out the best in each planet, but you must approach it with an open mind and learn to work with it. For example:

- If the Sun and Venus are in a semi-sextile aspect, it means the person will have difficulty finding balance in their relationships. They can struggle to accept love and express their emotions and will constantly feel on edge.
- On the other hand, if the Moon and Jupiter are in a semi-sextile aspect, it can mean the person is creative and optimistic. They may have an easier time expressing their emotions and be more willing to take risks and try new things.
- If the Sun is semi-sextile to the Moon, it shows a blend of compassion and assertiveness in the individual. This observation makes it easier for the astrologer to find a balance between their ambitions and emotions during a reading.
- If Venus is semi-sextile to Jupiter, it signifies how astrologers should encourage their clients to seek beauty and joy while staying grounded in reality.
- When Saturn is semi-sextile to Mercury, it helps astrologists apply a practical approach to communication.
- When Mars is semi-sextile to the Moon, it signifies a blend of aggression and receptiveness, allowing the expression of needs without being too pushy or aggressive.

The Quincunx

As a sign of growth or transformation, the quincunx aspect is considered an aspect of adjustment. Formed when two planets are 150 degrees apart (five signs apart) in the zodiac wheel, this oddly angled aspect is not found in any other aspect, so considered quite unique. Quincunxes can symbolize challenges or difficulties that must be overcome to progress in life. It is often a sign that some adjustment or transformation must happen to reach a certain goal. Depending on the planets involved, it could be a mental, emotional, physical, or spiritual adjustment. The quincunx is often:

- A sign of growth and evolution.
- A sign that a person is ready to move on to the next level but must make certain changes.
- A sign that a person is undergoing transformation and they must make adjustments to navigate the process successfully.

How Quincunx Work in the Charts

The quincunx aspect can show where to find balance and harmony. It can give insight into how to overcome difficulties and helps understand where people struggle.

- The Sun is the source of all life and energy, so a quincunx aspect can indicate a struggle to find balance or harmony in life.
- The Moon is associated with emotions and feelings, so a quincunx aspect can indicate difficulty expressing feelings or finding emotional balance.
- Venus is the planet of love and relationships, so a quincunx aspect can indicate a lack of harmony in relationships.
- Jupiter is the planet of expansion and good fortune, so a quincunx aspect can indicate a struggle to find success or abundance.
- Saturn is the planet of limitation and restriction, so a quincunx aspect can indicate difficulty in achieving goals or finding stability.
- Mercury is the planet of communication, so a quincunx aspect can indicate a struggle with communication or expressing yourself.
- Mars is the planet of action and energy, so a quincunx aspect can indicate difficulty in taking action or finding motivation.

The Quintile

The quintile aspect is created when two planets are separated by 72 degrees. This angle creates energy between the two planets, which can be positive and negative. Astrologers believe it to be especially beneficial for creative and intuitive endeavors. It signifies a strong connection between the planets, allowing a greater understanding of each individual and a more powerful creative force. The energies associated with the quintile help attain success and achieve ambitions.

- It emphasizes taking advantage of opportunities, as it encourages being open to new experiences and taking risks.
- It notifies positive energy, and astrologers often recommend it to their clients as a way to move forward in life. They will suggest the client meditate on the energies associated with the quintile and use them to create positive change and success.
- Besides bringing luck, it can open up new opportunities, so astrologers might suggest their clients take advantage of these opportunities.

How Quintile Work in the Charts

When the five planets in a quintile are in their respective positions, they form a pentagram. Each point of the pentagram is connected to a different planet. The Sun is connected to the base point, the Moon to the top point, Venus to the left point, Jupiter to the right point, and Saturn to the upper middle point. This pentagram influences the energies of each planet. Together the planets of a quintile are acknowledged as a spiritual aspect. They serve as a bridge between the physical and the spiritual worlds. For example:

- The Sun is the most affected by the quintile aspect, bringing an intense focus, energy, and ambition to the person's life.
- The Moon is associated with emotional intensity, a deeper understanding of relationships, and increased intuition.
- Venus promotes joy and pleasure, a greater appreciation of beauty, and increased charisma.
- Jupiter symbolizes luck, wealth, and increased optimism.
- Saturn is associated with greater responsibility, discipline, and practicality.

The Bi-Quintile

The bi-quintile is a relatively lesser-known planetary aspect in astrology. The 144-degree aspect with unique associated energy can manifest creative and innovative solutions to problems. The bi-quintile is considered one of the most creative aspects of astrology because it brings out the best in a person and helps them manifest their dreams and aspirations. The bi-quintile can also:

- Promote thinking outside the box and creating creative solutions to problems.
- Help a person find a unique approach to a situation.
- Manifest positive changes in a person's life.

The bi-quintile has spiritual energy associated with it. This aspect allows a person to tap into the spiritual realm and receive guidance and insight into matters related to their spiritual path. Besides helping a person connect to their higher self, it can give them clarity and insight into their lives.

How Bi-Quintile Work in the Charts

The bi-quintile aspect is a relatively rare astrological aspect, often overlooked in favor of more traditional aspects, like the conjunction, trine, and square. This harmonious aspect is usually associated with two planets in a supportive relationship.

The Sun, Moon, Mercury, Mars, Venus, Saturn, and Jupiter create the bi-quintile aspect. The Sun and Moon are the most important planets in this aspect. When the Sun and Moon form a bi-quintile, it is a favorable time for making important decisions and finding harmony and balance.

- Venus and Jupiter, in a bi-quintile aspect, bring the potential for great luck and abundance. It is an ideal time for taking risks with investments, starting a new business, or expanding creative endeavors.
- Saturn and Mercury, in a bi-quintile aspect, are beneficial for business transactions and negotiations. These two planets can potentially push learning new skills or gaining knowledge.
- In a bi-quintile aspect, Mars and Venus can help find balance in relationships. It indicates the suggestion to make compromises,

find a middle ground, and take the right path.

The Semi-Square

The semi-square is a very subtle aspect and can be quite challenging to handle because it is rarely used in traditional astrology. Formed at a 45-degree angle between two planets, representing tension, conflict, and discord, astrologers can still use this aspect to help understand a person's challenges, blocks, and obstacles. The person might be prone to conflict and misunderstandings in relationships. When astrologers consider the semi-square aspect, they look at the planets it affects. The planets provide insight into what conflicts and obstacles the individual is facing. For example:

- If the semi-square aspect affects the planet of relationships, then it can indicate the person is struggling in their relationships.
- If the semi-square aspect affects the planet of career, then it indicates the person experiences difficulty in their career.

Astrologers must also consider the planets' sign to gain a deeper understanding of the semi-square aspect. For example:

If the planets are in an often difficult or challenging sign, then the semi-square aspect will be even more pronounced.

How Semi-Square Work in the Charts

The semi-square aspect is one of the most potent astrological configurations and can strongly influence how planets interact. It creates a powerful connection between the planets and in the horoscope as a ray of energy connecting them. The Sun, Moon, Venus, Jupiter, Saturn, Mercury, and Mars all have the potential to be connected by a semi-square aspect. When two of these planets form a semi-square, the energy between them is quite intense, and the effects can be felt in the individuals' lives.

- The Sun is the source of all power in astrology, and when connected by a semi-square, it can bring a strong personal power.
- When a semi-square connects with the Moon, it can trigger powerful emotions and cause the individual to be more sensitive to external influences.

- Venus is the planet of love and relationships, and when connected by a semi-square, it can create strong attraction and desire.
- Jupiter is the planet of luck and fortune, and when connected by a semi-square, it can produce positive changes and unexpected opportunities.
- Saturn is the planet of limitations, and when connected by a semi-square, it can bring restriction and blockage.
- Mercury is the planet of communication and intellect, and when connected by a semi-square, it can facilitate a better understanding of ideas and concepts.
- Mars is the planet of aggression and action, and when connected by a semi-square, it can evoke impatience and a need for quick action.

The Sesquiquadrate (Sesquisquare)

Astrologers use the sesquiquadrate aspect to identify potential areas of tension and friction in a person's life. A sesquiquadrate aspect is formed on the birth chart when two planets are separated by a 135-degree angle. The sesquiquadrate aspect is a relatively minor influence in a birth chart but can still have a significant impact. It indicates a conflict between the two planets and a need for adjustment to bring the two energies into harmony. Essentially, it is a warning sign of potential problems and challenges. For example, it indicates the reconciliation of different parts of yourselves or resolving conflicts between your internal and external worlds.

Often described as a "crisis of transformation," it can force people to confront difficult issues and make difficult decisions. It brings inner conflict and can make it difficult for the person to decide, leading to anxiety, fear, and worry.

How Sesquisquare Work in the Charts

The sesquisquare aspect can be formed between the Sun, Moon, Venus, Jupiter, Saturn, Mercury, and Mars, although it commonly involves the Sun and Moon.

As the most important planet in the solar system, the Sun gives each individual a purpose and identity. The Sun's sesquisquare aspect can bring intense development in the individual's life because it is associated with life-giving energy.

- The sesquisquare aspect of the Moon signifies a period of inner exploration and reflection. There might be a need to examine a person's inner psyche and look within. It can be a time of great healing and transformation as the individual works through their emotional blocks.
- The sesquisquare aspect of Venus indicates a period of romantic and creative exploration. A person might want to connect with others and express themself meaningfully. It can create a heightened appreciation for beauty and the finer things in life.
- The sesquisquare aspect of Jupiter suggests a period of growth and opportunity. As a result, there could be a need to take risks and trust in life's process. Jupiter is known as the planet of luck and fortune, so it can show a period of luck and opportunity.
- The sesquisquare aspect of Saturn signifies a period of hard work and dedication. It can be a time when the individual is challenged to face their fears and take responsibility for their actions. Individuals might have to be honest with themselves and stay disciplined during this time.

Astrologers use minor aspects to add further depth to a horoscope. These planetary aspects are subtle but can give greater insight into the individual's character. Minor aspects uncover hidden traits, tendencies, and potentials not as apparent when looking at the major aspects alone. While the major aspects focus on the more straightforward and obvious elements, the minor aspects provide a more nuanced understanding. For example, suppose the minor aspects reveal a person to be more emotionally sensitive than previously thought. In that case, the astrologer can suggest ways to help the individual cope with their sensitivity. Minor aspects are invaluable for astrologers as they provide invaluable insights into their clients' lives.

Chapter 9: Planetary Transits

As you know by now, horary astrology deals with answering specific questions by interpreting the positions of the planets and stars at the moment a question is asked. How a planet moves can paint a clearer picture of the answer sought by the horary astrologer. One of the critical factors in understanding these movements is the concept of planetary transits. Planetary transits are crucial in horary astrology, as they help the astrologer interpret the current state of affairs and predict what will likely occur. By understanding planetary transits, the astrologer can predict the movement of the planets in the future and, therefore, anticipate the possible events that could occur.

Understanding the significance of planetary transits is imperative if you are a student of horary astrology. It is not enough to merely read a chart and interpret its meaning without considering the movements of the planets. Planetary transits provide valuable information to help you interpret horary readings accurately and gain insight into the future. This chapter explores the concept of planetary transits in more detail. By the end of this chapter, you'll have a comprehensive understanding of planetary transits and their significance in horary astrology. You can apply this knowledge to your readings and gain a deeper insight into current affairs and possible future events.

Planetary Transits vs. Aspects

In horary astrology, the concept of planetary transits is particularly important. Horary astrology deals with interpreting the planet's and star's positions at the moment a specific question is asked, aiming to provide answers and insights into the situation. Planetary transits in horary astrology refer to the current movement of the planets through the zodiac and their relationship to the planets and houses in the horary chart. Each planet's transit through a particular sign and house provides valuable information about the current state of affairs and the possible future outcome of the situation being questioned.

For example, if a person asks a horary question about their financial situation. The astrologer may look at Jupiter's current position, the planet associated with wealth and abundance, and its transit through the houses and signs of the chart to gain insight into the person's financial prospects. Unlike aspects, which focus on the relationship between two planets at a specific moment, planetary transits provide a broader context for understanding the planet's movement and influence. By looking at the broader patterns and movements of the planets, astrologers can gain a deeper understanding of the energies and influences shaping the situation.

While both planetary transits and aspects are important concepts in astrology, they have distinct differences in their focus and interpretation. Planetary transits focus on the planets' current movement through the zodiac and their relationship to the houses and signs of the chart. This movement occurs over a longer period, days, weeks, or even months, depending on the planet and its orbit's length. Aspects provide a snapshot of the current planetary relationships, whereas planetary transits provide a broader context for understanding the planets' movement and influence. Transits can indicate major themes or changes likely to occur in a person's life, while aspects provide more specific information about the energies and influences in a particular situation.

Another difference between planetary transits and aspects is the frequency of their occurrence. Aspects occur relatively frequently, sometimes several times a day, while planetary transits are rarer and occur over a longer period. So, while aspects can provide information about shorter-term influences and energies, planetary transits can offer insight into more significant long-term trends and themes. Overall, both planetary transits and aspects are important tools in the astrologer's toolkit and can be used together to gain a more comprehensive understanding of a person's life and the energies and influences. Astrologers can provide more accurate and insightful readings for their clients by understanding these differences.

Mutual Reception

Mutual reception is an astrological term referring to a unique relationship between two planets in each other's signs of rulership. This occurs when two planets are in signs ruled by the other planet, creating a connection between them that can enhance their energies. For example, Venus is in Scorpio, and Mars is in Libra. In this case, Venus is in Mars's sign of rulership (because Mars rules Scorpio), while Mars is in Venus's sign of rulership (because Venus rules Libra). This creates a mutual reception between the two planets, indicating a harmonious connection and the potential for increased energy and productivity.

The astrological process of mutual reception occurs when two planets are in each other's signs of rulership. This creates a unique energy that can amplify both planets' influence and produce positive results. In the example above, Venus in Scorpio and Mars in Libra would be in mutual reception, as they are in each other's signs of rulership. When planets are in mutual reception, they can work together more integrated and powerfully, leading to increased energy, productivity, and harmony in the areas of life ruled by those planets. For example, suppose Venus and Mars were in mutual reception. It could indicate a positive and productive time for relationships and partnerships, as Venus rules love and relationships while Mars rules action and energy.

Mutual reception is a relatively rare occurrence in astrology, as it requires two planets to be in each other's signs of rulership. However, it can be a powerful and positive influence when it does occur. When each planet goes through this process can vary depending on the planets' specific positions and the signs they are in. However, astrologers can use software or ephemerides to calculate the exact dates and times when mutual reception occurs based on the planet's movements through the zodiac. Overall, mutual reception is a valuable tool for astrologers to interpret horary charts and gain insights into the planets' unique relationships.

Other examples of mutual reception can include:

1. Venus in Scorpio and Mars in Libra

In this case, Venus is in Scorpio, ruled by Mars, and Mars is in Libra, ruled by Venus. This is a commonly occurring example of mutual reception. When these particular planets are in mutual reception, they can be found in each other's specific home sign. It allows them to work together harmoniously and express their energies more effectively.

In this case, Venus in Scorpio can access the powerful and transformative energy of Mars, helping Venus express its desire for intimacy and emotional depth more effectively. On the other hand, Mars in Libra can benefit from Venus's diplomatic and harmonizing energy, helping Mars express its assertiveness and take action more effectively. This placement might suggest a relationship where both partners understand and appreciate each other's needs and desires.

2. Mercury in Pisces and Neptune in Gemini

When Mercury and Neptune are in mutual reception, it means each planet is in the sign ruled by the other planet. In this case, Mercury is in Pisces (which Neptune rules), and Neptune is in Pisces (which Neptune *also rules*). This placement can profoundly impact your mental state and perception of reality. Mercury governs communication, learning, and logical thinking, while Neptune represents intuition, spirituality, and the subconscious. When the two planets are in mutual reception, their energies can work together, creating a period of heightened intuition and sensitivity.

People are more in tune with their inner voice and the world around them during this time. Their dreams and inner visions might be more vivid, and they might be drawn to creative pursuits, such as writing, art, or music. Simultaneously, this placement can make them more prone to escapism and daydreaming, so they must be mindful of staying grounded and in reality.

3. Jupiter in Aries and Mars in Sagittarius

Jupiter and Mars in mutual reception means Jupiter is in Aries (the sign ruled by Mars), while Mars is in the sign ruled by Jupiter (Sagittarius). This mutual reception creates a positive and harmonious energy between these two planets and has several implications. Firstly, Jupiter is the planet of expansion, growth, and optimism, while Mars is the planet of action, passion, and drive. When these two planets are in mutual reception, it can indicate a period of increased energy and enthusiasm, especially in pursuing goals and taking risks. People may feel more confident and willing to take on challenges and try new things during this time.

Secondly, this placement can indicate when a person feels confident to make decisions and take action. Jupiter's influence can bring a sense of faith and trust in a person's abilities, while Mars' influence can provide the drive and motivation to act on those beliefs. It can be a favorable time to start new projects, take on leadership roles, and pursue passions. Overall, Jupiter and Mars, in mutual reception, can bring harmony and balance between expansion and action, faith and drive, leading to a productive and fulfilling period.

Planets in Retrograde

Retrograde motion in astrology refers to the apparent backward motion of a planet observed from Earth. This occurs due to differences in the orbital speed and distance of the planets and the Earth's orbital motion. If a planet is in retrograde, it will appear to move in a backward direction through the zodiac. However, this is just an illusion caused when the Earth passes a slower-moving planet in its orbit. During this period, the planet's energy is thought to turn inward, causing people to reflect on the themes associated with that planet. Each planet goes through this process at different times and for different durations. Mercury, Venus, Mars, Jupiter, and Saturn experience retrograde periods.

1. Mercury Retrograde

Mercury retrograde is perhaps the most well-known retrograde period in astrology. This event occurs approximately three times yearly and lasts about three weeks. As with any retrograde event, the planet, in this case, Mercury, appears to move backward through the zodiac. Mercury is associated with communication, technology, transportation, and travel. Therefore, these areas can be affected when it goes retrograde, and challenges can arise. Common experiences during Mercury retrograde include communication breakdowns, technical glitches, delays, and misunderstandings.

Mercury retrograde can affect specific areas; communication is perhaps the most significant. It can be when misunderstandings and miscommunications are more likely to occur, leading to problems in personal and professional relationships and delays in getting things done. Technology and transportation can be affected during Mercury retrograde. It is not uncommon for computers to crash, phones to break, and cars to break down during this period. Therefore, it might be best to back up important files and avoid making major technology purchases or scheduling important trips during this time.

2. Venus Retrograde

Venus retrograde is considered to be comparatively rare and only occurs every 19 months, lasting about 6 weeks. During this period, Venus appears to move backward through the zodiac, impacting various aspects of life, like love, relationships, beauty, art, and values. Therefore, when it goes into retrograde, these areas can be affected, and challenges can arise. You may experience a range of emotions related to personal relationships. It can be a time when old flames return or past relationships resurface. However, remember these might not necessarily be opportunities for reconciliation or rekindling a relationship.

Venus retrograde is a time for introspection and reflection on your values and self-worth. It is a good time to question your beliefs about love and beauty and reevaluate whether they serve you. For creative endeavors, Venus retrograde can be a time to revisit past projects or reevaluate your artistic vision. It is a time to review what you have created and assess whether it aligns with your current creative goals.

3. Mars Retrograde

Mars retrograde takes place every two years, during which the planet Mars seems to move backward in its orbit. During Mars retrograde, the planet's energy is intensified and can significantly impact astrological readings and interpretations. Mars is associated with drive, ambition, and assertiveness. So, when it goes retrograde, many feel frustrated or blocked in their efforts to pursue their goals, leading to restlessness, impatience, lashing out, or impulsiveness.

On the positive side, Mars retrograde can be a time for introspection and self-reflection. It can be an opportunity to slow down, re-evaluate priorities, and reflect on actions and decisions. It could be a time for resolving conflicts and working on communication skills. Those with Aries or Scorpio in their birth chart might be particularly affected by Mars retrograde, as Mars is the ruling planet of both signs. These signs may experience heightened emotions, conflicts, and challenges during this time.

4. Saturn Retrograde

Saturn retrograde happens approximately once every year and lasts for around four and a half months. When Saturn goes into retrograde, you may feel pressure, particularly where you have been neglecting your responsibilities or where you need to take more accountability. Saturn retrograde can be a time for self-reflection and reevaluating your long-term goals and plans.

Those with Capricorn or Aquarius in their birth chart may be particularly affected by Saturn retrograde, as these signs are ruled by Saturn. During this time, these signs may experience greater responsibility and pressure in their professional and personal lives.

5. Jupiter Retrograde

Jupiter retrograde occurs yearly for a comparatively longer period than other retrograde events, lasting about four months. Jupiter is associated with expansion, growth, and abundance. When Jupiter goes into retrograde, people feel contraction – particularly where they have been over-indulging or overextending themselves. Those with Sagittarius or Pisces in their birth chart may be particularly affected by Jupiter retrograde, as they are ruled by Jupiter. During this time, these signs could experience greater introspection and inner growth and a focus on their spiritual and philosophical development.

Overall, retrograde periods are considered times for reflection, review, and reassessment rather than for initiating new projects or making major changes. Being mindful of the energy of the retrograde planet during these periods and using the time wisely for personal growth and introspection is important.

When Planets Combust

In horary astrology, the *combustion of a planet* occurs when a planet is within 8.5 degrees of the Sun and is considered a significant condition affecting the interpretation of a horary chart. When a planet is in combustion, its significators become weakened. The heat and light of the Sun can overpower the qualities and attributes of the planet, making it harder for the planet to function effectively. The planets most commonly affected by combustion are Mercury and Venus, as they are the closest planets to the Sun. However, all planets can go through a combustion period, depending on their distance from the Sun and their position in the zodiac.

When a planet is in combustion, it is "under the beams" of the Sun. As the planet moves closer to the Sun, it becomes increasingly weakened and might not deliver its results. The effects of combustion can last for different periods, depending on the planet and its position in the zodiac. The planet's significators might not manifest as strongly as usual. There could be delays, obstacles, or challenges with the planet's significators.

The planet's position in the horary chart, its aspect to other planets, and the house it rules should be considered to understand its impact on the chart.

When Mercury is in combustion, it can affect communication, intelligence, and logical thinking. Mercury represents communication, learning, and exchange of information, and when it is in combustion, it leads to misunderstandings, delays in communication, and difficulty in comprehending information. It affects technology, transportation, and travel, as Mercury rules these areas. During this period, it is advisable to be extra careful in communication and avoid making important decisions requiring a clear understanding of information.

When Venus is in combustion, it can affect relationships, love, and creativity. Venus represents social relationships, romantic connections, and artistic expression. When Venus is in combustion, there could be challenges in these areas, like misunderstandings, disagreements, or delays. It may affect matters of finance, luxury items, and beauty. During this period, it is advisable to be cautious in relationships and avoid making important financial decisions or big purchases of luxury items.

Planetary transits in horary astrology are like cosmic traffic signals, providing valuable information about the universe's energetic flow and how it influences people's lives. Like a skilled driver, a skilled astrologer can use this information to navigate the twists and turns of life, avoiding roadblocks and finding the smoothest path to their destination. Whether you seek clarity on a specific question or merely deepen your understanding of the cosmic dance, planetary transits offer a fascinating and illuminating lens through which to view the mysteries of the universe.

Chapter 10: How to Read Any Horary Chart

You've reached the final chapter of your exploration into the world of horary astrology. It's time to put your learned knowledge and skills to the test. You've learned about the symbols and meanings of the planets, houses, aspects, and planetary transits. Now, it's time to take the next step and learn to read a horary chart to find the answers you seek. Horary astrology is a unique form of divination requiring a specific moment and a clear question to work effectively. It's like tuning into a specific frequency on a radio - you need the right time and place to access the information you seek. However, unlike other forms of divination, horary astrology is not about changing the outcome to fit your desires. It's about gaining insight and understanding into a situation and discovering the best path forward.

Interpreting a horary chart can be challenging and complex, but with practice and patience, it can be a powerful tool for gaining clarity and decision-making. It requires a keen eye for detail, an open mind, and trust in the symbols and signs. By learning to read a horary chart, you can access a pearl of deeper wisdom and guidance available at the moment. This chapter highlights the key concepts and techniques for interpreting a horary chart, providing step-by-step instructions and plenty of examples to help you get started. So, start exploring the mysteries of the universe and discover what the stars have in store for you.

Creating a Horary Chart

Creating a Horary Chart requires noting the exact time, location, and question being asked. To create a horary chart, follow these steps:

1. Determine the exact time, location, and question being asked. Ensure the time is noted as accurately as possible, including the seconds, and it is the local time of the person asking the question. The location of the person asking the question is important as it provides information for determining the ascendant and the houses of the chart. Additionally, the question should be clear and specific to allow precise chart interpretation.
2. Use an ephemeris to determine the positions of the planets and luminaries (Sun and Moon) at the exact time and location of the question. An ephemeris is a table or book listing the celestial bodies' positions at different times. You can find an ephemeris online or in a book.
3. Determine the ascendant by using the location and time of the question. It is the sign rising on the eastern horizon when the question is asked. You can use an online calculator or refer to an ephemeris to determine the ascendant.
4. Draw a chart with the ascendant on the left and the other signs in the same order as they appear in the zodiac. The chart should have 12 houses, with the first house starting at the ascendant and proceeding in a counterclockwise direction.
5. Place the planets and luminaries in the appropriate houses of the chart based on their positions when the question is asked. The planets' positions are indicated in the ephemeris. For example, if Mars were in the sign of Taurus at the time of the question, it would be placed in the second house of the chart (corresponding to Taurus).
6. Consider the planetary aspects (angles) and their meanings. Aspects are formed when planets are certain degrees apart and indicate positive or negative interactions between planets. You can use an online calculator or an ephemeris to determine the aspects between planets. You've already studied the planetary aspects in previous chapters, and

examples can include oppositions, conjunctions, or trines.
7. Interpret the chart based on traditional horary astrology principles, including the meanings of the houses, planets, and aspects. The chart interpretation is a complex process requiring knowledge of astrological symbolism and traditional principles of interpretation. You should seek guidance from an experienced astrologer if you are unfamiliar with these principles.

Alternatively, online horary chart calculators and software can create a chart based on input information. These can be helpful for beginners not familiar with astrological symbolism. However, the chart's accuracy generated by software or calculators can vary, depending on the program quality and the data's accuracy.

Example 1:

Let's use an example to better explain the creation of a horary chart. For this example, a person asks whether they will get a job offer for the specific position they applied for. Here are the steps to follow:

1. Determine the exact time, location, and question: You asked the question on February 22, 2023, at 3:45 pm in Los Angeles, California. The asked question is, "Will I be able to get the position I applied for?"
2. Use an ephemeris to determine the positions of the planets and luminaries at the exact time and location of the question: Consulting an ephemeris at 3:45 pm in Los Angeles on February 22, 2023, the positions of the planets and luminaries are as follows:
    o Sun: 4 degrees Pisces
    o Moon: 18 degrees Virgo
    o Mercury: 11 degrees Aquarius
    o Venus: 2 degrees Pisces
    o Mars: 16 degrees Capricorn
    o Jupiter: 11 degrees Pisces
    o Saturn: 9 degrees Aquarius
    o Uranus: 9 degrees Taurus
3. Determine the ascendant: To determine the ascendant, you must know the exact time and location of the question. Using

an online calculator or an ephemeris, the ascendant at 3:45 pm in Los Angeles on February 22, 2023, is 14 degrees Scorpio.

4. Draw the chart: you can use software or draw the chart by hand. The chart should have the ascendant on the left, and the signs must be in the same order as they appear in the zodiac. The chart will have 12 houses, with the first house starting at the ascendant and proceeding counterclockwise. The exact position of each house in this chart is:
   - First House (ascendant): Scorpio
   - Second House: Sagittarius
   - Third House: Capricorn
   - Fourth House: Aquarius
   - Fifth House: Pisces
   - Sixth House: Aries
   - Seventh House: Taurus
   - Eighth House: Gemini
   - Ninth House: Cancer
   - Tenth House: Leo
   - Eleventh House: Virgo
   - Twelfth House: Libra

5. Place the planets and luminaries in the appropriate houses of the chart: Place them in the appropriate houses of the chart using the planets' and luminaries' positions. For example, the Moon is in the sixth house, Venus is in the first house, and Mars is in the ninth house.

6. Consider the planetary aspects. You can use an online calculator or an ephemeris to determine the planetary aspects. For example, Mars may be forming a sextile aspect (60 degrees) with Jupiter, which is in the eleventh house.

7. Interpret the chart: Interpreting the chart requires knowledge of traditional principles of horary astrology, including the meanings of the houses, planets, and aspects you've learned from this book.

Example 2:

A person asks whether they should buy a particular car they've been eyeing. Here are the steps to follow:

1. Determine the exact time, location, and question: The person asked the question on March 10, 2023, at 10:30 am in Miami, Florida. The question is, "Should I buy the blue Toyota Camry I saw at the dealership yesterday?"
2. Use an ephemeris to determine the planets' and luminaries' positions at the exact time and location of the question: Consulting an ephemeris at 10:30 am in Miami on March 10, 2023, the positions of the planets and luminaries are as follows:
    o Sun: 19 degrees Pisces
    o Moon: 5 degrees Capricorn
    o Mercury: 27 degrees Aquarius
    o Venus: 28 degrees Aquarius
    o Mars: 16 degrees Taurus
    o Jupiter: 16 degrees Pisces
    o Saturn: 8 degrees Aquarius
    o Uranus: 14 degrees Taurus
3. Determine the ascendant: To determine the ascendant, you must know the exact time and location of the question. Using an online calculator or an ephemeris, the ascendant at 10:30 am in Miami on March 10, 2023, is 22 degrees Cancer.
4. Draw the chart: You can use software or draw the chart by hand. The chart should have the ascendant on the left, and the signs must be in the same order as they appear in the zodiac. The chart has 12 houses, with the first house starting at the ascendant and proceeding counterclockwise. The exact position of each house in this chart is:
    o First House (ascendant): Cancer
    o Second House: Leo
    o Third House: Virgo
    o Fourth House: Libra
    o Fifth House: Scorpio

- Sixth House: Sagittarius
- Seventh House: Capricorn
- Eighth House: Aquarius
- Ninth House: Pisces
- Tenth House: Aries
- Eleventh House: Taurus
- Twelfth House: Gemini

5. Place the planets and luminaries in the appropriate houses of the chart: Place them in the appropriate houses of the chart using the planets' and luminaries' positions. For example, the Moon is in the third house, Venus is in the third house, and Mars is in the ninth house.
6. Consider the planetary aspects: You can use an online calculator or an ephemeris to determine the planetary aspects. For example, Mars may be forming a trine aspect (120 degrees) with Uranus, which is in the ninth house.
7. Interpret the chart: Interpreting the chart requires knowledge of traditional principles of horary astrology, including the meanings of the houses, planets, and aspects you've learned from this book.

The next section discusses the interpretation of a horary chart in more detail.

Interpreting a Horary Chart

Interpreting a horary chart is a complex and nuanced process requiring a deep understanding of astrology principles and an ability to synthesize information from different areas of the chart. The horary chart is a snapshot of the moment the question was asked and provides insight into the querent's motivations, the situation, and its potential outcome. When you want to interpret a horary chart in detail, you must consider the position of the planets, the signs and houses they occupy, and even their relationship to one another. Each placement and aspect provide a piece of the puzzle. So, viewing the chart as a whole is essential for a meaningful and helpful interpretation. With careful analysis and interpretation, a horary chart can provide valuable insight and guidance to the querent. Here are detailed steps for interpreting a horary chart:

1. **Identify the primary significator:** The primary significator is the planet ruling the house representing the question. For example, if the question concerns a job, the tenth house would represent the question, and its ruling planet, Saturn, would be the primary significator.
2. **Look for the secondary significators:** The secondary significators are the planets with a special connection to the question or querent. For example, the Moon represents the querent, and planets in the same sign or house as the Moon would be secondary significators.
3. **Consider the position and aspects of the primary *significator*:** The position and aspects of the primary significator provide essential information about the question's answer. For example, if Saturn is in a favorable aspect with Venus, this could indicate a positive outcome about the job.
4. **Look for interceptions and void, of course, planets: Interceptions occur when a sign is intercepted within a house.** They can indicate hidden or delayed outcomes about the question. Void-of-course planets do not make any major aspects before they are supposed to leave their occupied sign. They can indicate delays or lack of progress on the question.
5. **Consider the position and aspects of the Moon:** The position and aspects of the Moon provide information about the querent's emotional state and involvement in the situation. For example, if the Moon is in a favorable aspect with the primary significator, this could indicate the querent is in an excellent position to achieve the desired outcome.
6. **Look for accidental dignities:** Accidental dignities are factors influencing the strength or weakness of a planet in a chart. For example, if a planet is in its own sign, in a favorable aspect with a benefic planet, or in the same sign as the ascendant, it could be considered strong.
7. **Look for the final dispositor:** A final dispositor is the planet with the most power in a chart due to being in charge of other planets through various house placements. For example, if Mars is the final dispositor of the chart, its influence would be heightened.

8. **Consider the chart as a whole:** It is essential to view the chart as a whole and consider all the factors discussed above when interpreting a horary chart. An experienced astrologer can provide more in-depth and nuanced analysis.

Overall, interpreting a horary chart can be a complex process requiring a good understanding of astrology principles and an ability to synthesize information from different areas of the chart. Anyone seeking to interpret a horary chart consulting an experienced astrologer is recommended.

An interpretation of the first example chart discussed above will look like this:

1. **Identify the primary significator:** The primary significator can be identified by considering a few factors. The tenth house represents the job, and its ruling planet is Jupiter, so Jupiter is the primary significator.
2. **Look for the secondary significators:** The Moon represents the querent, so it is a secondary significator. In this chart, the Moon is in the same sign as Jupiter, indicating a strong connection between the querent and the job.
3. **Consider the position and aspects of the primary significator:** Jupiter is in the sign of Capricorn and, in the eleventh house, a favorable position for job-related matters. Jupiter is in close conjunction with Venus, which represents harmony and positive outcomes. These factors suggest a positive outcome for the querent about the job.
4. **Look for interceptions and void-of-course planets:** This chart has no interceptions or void-of-course planets.
5. **Consider the position and aspects of the Moon:** The Moon is in the sign of Capricorn, which is the same sign as Jupiter, indicating a strong connection between the querent and the job. The Moon is in a favorable aspect with Jupiter and Venus, which further indicates a positive outcome about the job.
6. **Look for accidental dignities:** Jupiter is in its own sign, a strong accidental dignity, and is in a favorable aspect with Venus, another benefic planet, further strengthening Jupiter's position in the chart.

7. **Look for the final dispositor:** Jupiter is the final dispositor of the chart, as it is the ruler of the ascendant and the house representing the job. It indicates that Jupiter has a strong influence and power over the chart.
8. **Consider the chart as a whole:** Overall, the chart suggests a positive outcome for the querent about the job. Jupiter, the primary significator, is in a strong and favorable position, and the Moon, representing the querent, is well-aspect. No significant negative factors are present in the chart, which further supports a positive outcome. However, astrology is not deterministic, so there could be other factors that cannot be fully captured in the chart.

An interpretation for the second example (a person inquiring whether they should purchase a car) would have these steps:

1. **Identify the primary significator:** The question pertains to purchasing a car, which falls under the domain of the second house. The ruling planet of the second house is Venus, so Venus is the primary significator.
2. **Look for the secondary significators:** The Moon represents the querent, and planets in the same sign or house as the Moon would be secondary significators.
3. **Consider the position and aspects of the primary significator:** Venus is in Aries in the ninth house, which suggests the person is enthusiastic and eager about the idea of buying the car. Venus is in a square aspect with Mars in Capricorn, indicating potential obstacles or conflicts about the purchase.
4. **Look for interceptions and void-of-course planets:** This chart has no interceptions or void-of-course planets.
5. **Consider the position and aspects of the Moon:** The Moon is in Gemini in the fourth house, suggesting the querent is curious and seeking information about the car. The Moon is in a square aspect, with Neptune in Pisces in the third house, indicating confusion or deception around the purchase.
6. **Look for accidental dignities:** Venus is in its own sign of Aries, a positive factor indicating strength and potency.
7. **Look for the final dispositor:** Jupiter is the final dispositor in this chart, as it rules the Moon in Gemini and Venus in

Aries.

8. **Consider the chart as a whole:** The chart suggests that while the person is excited about the prospect of buying the car, there could be some conflicts that must be addressed before the purchase is finalized. The Moon's aspect with Neptune suggests confusion or deception around the purchase. Therefore, the person should gather more information before deciding.

Creating and interpreting a horary chart can be a complex process. Still, with the knowledge and techniques you've learned in this chapter, you are well on your way to becoming an adept practitioner of horary astrology. Remember, take time to carefully consider the question, consult an ephemeris, and draw the chart accurately. As you interpret the chart, pay attention to the relationships between the planets, houses, and aspects. Always refer to previous chapters and the glossary to quickly identify various glyphs and symbols in the chart. You can become proficient in this ancient and powerful divinatory art with practice and dedication.

Glossary of Terms and Glyphs

Zodiacs

Aries (♈) - Aries is the first sign in the zodiac and represents self-initiative, energy, courage, and leadership. It is symbolized by the Ram, a creature that charges forward aggressively, representing its assertive nature.

Taurus (♉) - Taurus is an earth sign focusing on material gain and stability. The Bull glyph associated with this sign reflects its stubbornness and patience while pursuing what it desires.

Gemini (♊) - Gemini is an air sign represented by two figures of twins connected at the head. This connection symbolizes communication and duality, which are characteristic qualities of a Gemini individual.

Cancer (♋) - Cancer is a water sign, and its glyph is the Crab which symbolizes instinctive reactions, protectiveness, and sensitivity. This sign rules the home and emotions making it very nurturing in nature.

Leo (♌) - Leo is a fire sign represented by the Lion, a creature that exhibits strength, courage, loyalty, and wisdom. It is an extroverted sign focusing on playfulness and creativity.

Virgo (♍) - Virgo is an earth sign represented by the Virgin, who symbolizes purity of heart and mind. This sign has analytical tendencies and focuses on details, especially when it comes to problem-solving tasks.

Libra (♎) – Libra is an air sign represented by the Scales, which symbolizes balance and justice. This sign is diplomatic in nature, always striving to reach harmony in any situation.

Scorpio (♏) – Scorpio is a water sign, and its glyph is the Scorpion which symbolizes strength of character and an ability to survive and overcome obstacles. It has a mysterious aura around it as it is considered one of the most intense signs in the zodiac.

Sagittarius (♐) – Sagittarius is a fire sign represented by an Archer that symbolizes courage, optimism, a freedom-loving spirit, and enthusiasm for life. A Sagittarian individual loves adventures and exploring new places.

Capricorn (♑) – Capricorn is an earth sign represented by the Goat, which symbolizes ambition, discipline, and hard work. This sign is practical in nature and takes a methodical approach to achieve its goals.

Aquarius (♒) – Aquarius is an air sign represented by the Water Bearer, which symbolizes knowledge, intelligence, and humanitarianism. An Aquarian individual loves to be around people but also needs plenty of alone time for introspection.

Pisces (♓) – Pisces is a water sign represented by two Fish swimming in opposite directions, one representing the spiritual world and the other representing the material world. A Piscean individual has sensitivity, imagination, and creativity as its main traits.

Alchemical Three Primes

Cardinal: This prime represents action, start, and movement. It is associated with the zodiac signs Aries, Cancer, Libra, and Capricorn and typically appears as an inverted triangle or arrowhead symbol in a horary chart. It reflects our ability to take the initiative and make decisions in order to achieve our goals.

Mutable: This prime signifies changeability and adaptability. It is associated with the zodiac signs Gemini, Virgo, Sagittarius, and Pisces and typically appears as a wave symbol in a horary chart. It reflects our ability to adjust to changing circumstances and adapt quickly to new situations.

Fixed: This prime represents stability and consistency. It is associated with the zodiac signs Taurus, Leo, Scorpio, and Aquarius and typically appears as a cross symbol in a horary chart. It reflects our ability to stay focused on our goals despite the potential for disruption or distraction.

Planets

Sun ☉: The Sun represents the conscious self, offering clarity on matters involving identity and purpose. It symbolizes vitality, creativity, and ambition. Its presence suggests taking action to manifest your desires and pursue new endeavors. The Sun's glyph looks like a circle with a dot in the center, representing its strong focus on goal achievement and creative expression.

Moon ☽: The Moon symbolizes the subconscious, providing insight into your unconscious motivations and emotions. This planet is associated with intuition, emotions, instinct, and unconscious desires. Its presence suggests exploring your inner depths and gaining a better understanding of you as a person. The Moon's glyph is shaped like a crescent moon, representing its connection to your emotional needs.

Mercury ☿: Mercury represents intellect and communication, helping make sense of the world through analysis and reason. It encourages curiosity, exploration, and learning new things. Its presence suggests paying closer attention to your thoughts and ideas to better understand yourself and the people around you. The Mercury glyph looks like a circle with a cross inside, symbolizing its ability to bring order out of chaos.

Venus ♀: Venus symbolizes love, beauty, and harmony. It encourages you to seek pleasure and comfort in your lives and appreciate the beauty around you. Its presence suggests enjoying life's luxuries and finding joy in simple pleasures. The Venus glyph looks like a circle with an arrow pointing up, symbolizing its connection to our capacity for love and appreciation.

Mars ♂: Mars represents energy, passion, and aggression. It helps you take action toward achieving your goals and overcoming obstacles. Its presence suggests taking decisive steps toward success instead of waiting passively for things to happen. The Mars glyph is shaped like an arrow pointing forward, representing its willingness to push ahead despite any challenges it may face.

Jupiter ♃: Jupiter symbolizes expansion and abundance, helping you grow and succeed in your endeavors. It encourages you to take risks, aim high and reach for the stars. Its presence suggests making the most out of opportunities that come your way. The Jupiter glyph looks like a four-pointed star, representing its ability to bring luck and success into our lives.

Saturn ♄: Saturn represents structure, discipline, and responsibility. It helps to create order in your life by setting boundaries and taking control of your environment. Its presence suggests creating rules and regulations in order to get things done effectively and efficiently. The Saturn glyph is shaped like a cross inside a circle, symbolizing its capacity to bring order out of chaos.

Uranus ⛢: Uranus symbolizes rebellion and disruption, helping to break free from oppressive environments and stand up for what you believe in. Its presence suggests taking bold actions to achieve your goals without being afraid of the consequences. The Uranus glyph looks like an inverted cross inside a circle, representing its capacity to overturn the status quo.

Neptune ♆: Neptune symbolizes intuition and spirituality, providing insight into unseen forces at work in our lives. It encourages us to explore our spiritual side and connect with higher powers. Its presence suggests trusting your instincts when making decisions. The Neptune glyph looks like two crescents overlapping each other, representing its ability to open us up to unseen realms of understanding.

Pluto ♇: Pluto represents transformation and rebirth, helping you confront your fears and make dramatic changes. Its presence suggests taking a hard look at yourselves and finding the courage to let go of old patterns that are no longer serving you. The Pluto glyph looks like an oval with a cross inside, symbolizing its capacity to help us break free from outdated ways of thinking.

Planetary Aspects

1. **Conjunction (☌):** This aspect occurs when two planets are in close proximity to each other, and their energies converge. It is usually interpreted as representing a union between both parties or an intensification of either one's energy, depending on the context.

2. **Opposition (☍):** This aspect occurs when two planets are 180 degrees apart from each other in relation to the Earth's position.

This usually suggests tension between two forces, conflict, and possibly even conflicting opinions or values.

3. **Square (□):** This aspect occurs when two planets are 90 degrees apart from each other in relation to the Earth's position. It is generally interpreted as representing obstacles or challenges that must be overcome for a successful outcome.

4. **Trine (♃):** This aspect occurs when two planets are 120 degrees apart from each other in relation to the Earth's position. It usually symbolizes harmony, balance, mutual understanding between two forces, and an opportunity for growth and development.

5. **Sextile (✱):** This aspect occurs when two planets are 60 degrees apart from each other in relation to the Earth's position. It often indicates potential opportunities or favorable conditions that may arise if one makes use of them.

6. **Quintile (◉):** This aspect occurs when two planets are 72 degrees apart from each other in relation to the Earth's position. It is usually interpreted as a hint or a clue that can lead one to uncover hidden potentials or latent abilities that may be beneficial if tapped into.

7. **Semisextile (△):** This aspect occurs when two planets are 30 degrees apart from each other in relation to the Earth's position. It often symbolizes subtle yet important changes or developments that could have far-reaching implications depending on how they are handled.

8. **Semisquare (△):** This aspect occurs when two planets are 45 degrees apart from each other in relation to the Earth's position. It usually suggests that one should take caution when making decisions or entering into agreements, as doing so may lead to complications.

9. **Sesquiquadrate (△):** This aspect occurs when two planets are 135 degrees apart from each other in relation to the Earth's position. Interpreted negatively, it can suggest blocked energy or difficulty in solving conflicts. However, looked at positively, it can indicate a need for greater effort and focus on a task or project for successful outcomes.

10. **Quincunx (⚻):** This aspect occurs when two planets are 150 degrees apart from each other in relation to the Earth's position. It typically symbolizes a need to compromise or adjust one's mindset in order to move forward. It can also indicate a potential solution if looked at from the right perspective.
11. **Parallel (||):** This aspect occurs when two planets are aligned with each other but not in exact conjunction. It usually suggests two forces working together towards common goals or objectives and the possibility of gaining insight on how best to reach those outcomes.

Angles

Ascendant A^{sc}: The Ascendant or Rising sign is the sign that was rising on the horizon at the exact moment of birth. It forms the eastern point in an astrological chart and can be thought of as a lens through which all energies travel, framing your behavior and attitude toward life. The glyph for this angle is a stylized figure of an arrow pointing up.

Midheaven M^c: This angle represents our ambition, career objectives, and public reputation. Its placement in a chart reveals how we may express ourselves to others, what kind of work suits us best, and how we will achieve success in life. The glyph for this angle looks like two inverted V's, one inside the other.

Vertex Vx: This angle is a kind of "fateful point," representing destiny, luck, and the power of fate. It often appears to be a coincidence or chance meeting that occurs at just the right time. The symbol for this angle looks like an inverted triangle with four lines coming out of it. Each line represents one side of the square that contains your lifetime journey. The vertex helps you make sense of these directions by understanding how they all interconnect and form a larger whole.

Conclusion

As you journey through the rich landscape of horary astrology, you discover that this ancient practice is as much an art as it is a science. The rules and guidelines provide a helpful framework, but your intuition, experience, and connection to the universe's energy ultimately guide you in interpreting the chart. You may tap into a pearl of deeper wisdom transcending astrology by learning this art.

By paying attention to the subtle signals and messages arising within and around you, you'll develop a heightened awareness and intuition to serve you well in all areas of your life. Whether you seek guidance on a particular issue or simply explore the vast expanse of astrological knowledge, the more you put into the practice, the more you'll get out of it.

At times, horary astrology might challenge you to confront difficult truths or make tough decisions. But with each reading, you'll gain a deeper understanding of yourself and the world around you and develop a greater appreciation for the complexity and beauty of life. As you practice horary astrology, approach each chart with reverence and respect. Remember, you are working with forces beyond your control; your role is to listen, observe, and respond with humility and grace.

This book has revealed the intricate dance between the planets and the zodiac and how these patterns offer insight into the questions weighing on your mind. But perhaps the greatest gift of horary astrology is not in the answers it provides but in the questions it inspires. By encouraging you to pause, reflect, and tune in to the universe's rhythms, horary astrology offers a powerful reminder of the interconnectedness of all things.

Always remember that horary astrology is a tool for growth and discovery, not a means of control or prediction. The chart offers valuable insight into a particular question or situation, but it is up to you to use the information to make choices aligning with your values and goals. Remember, horary astrology is only one tool in your toolbox. It offers valuable insight and guidance, but it is ultimately up to you to take ownership of your life and chart your path forward.

So, as you journey through the fascinating world of horary astrology, may you be guided by the star's wisdom, your intuition's power, and the universe's endless possibilities. Be inspired, motivated, and encouraged to live your best life using horary astrology as your ultimate guide.

Here's another book by Mari Silva that you might like

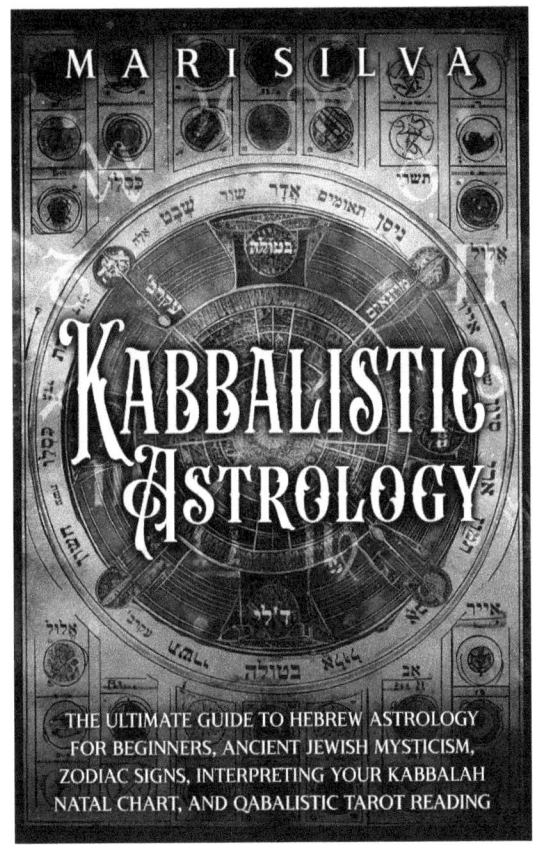

Your Free Gift
(only available for a limited time)

Thanks for getting this book! If you want to learn more about various spirituality topics, then join Mari Silva's community and get a free guided meditation MP3 for awakening your third eye. This guided meditation mp3 is designed to open and strengthen ones third eye so you can experience a higher state of consciousness. Simply visit the link below the image to get started.

https://spiritualityspot.com/meditation

References

(N.d.). Symbolspy.com. https://www.symbolspy.com/zodiac-symbols-text.html

"A Brief Introduction to Astrology: Aspects." n.d. Astro.com. . https://www.astro.com/astrology/in_aspect_e.htm.

"Aquarius Papers - Global Astrology." n.d. Aquarius Papers - Global Astrology. . https://www.aquariuspapers.com/astrology/2018/05/astrology-class-on-the-specializing-aspects-pt-1-the-quintile-and-biquintile.html.

"Horary Astrology Lesson 4, Aspects and Their Perfection." n.d. Tripod.com. . https://mithras93.tripod.com/lessons/lesson4/lesson4.html.

"Minor Aspects - Meaning." 2011. Astrologers' Community. February 13, 2011. https://www.astrologyweekly.com/forum/index.php?threads/minor-aspects-meaning.33323/.

"The Aspects." n.d. Astrograph.com. . https://www.astrograph.com/learning-astrology/aspects.php.

"The Aspects." n.d. Astrograph.com. . https://www.astrograph.com/learning-astrology/aspects.php.

"The Meaning of the Aspects in Astrology." 2015. Cafeastrology.com. Cafe Astrology .com. April 15, 2015. https://cafeastrology.com/articles/aspectsinastrology.html.

"The Most & Least Lucky Aspects to Have on Your Zodiac Chart, from Astrologers." 2022. Mindbodygreen. April 19, 2022. https://www.mindbodygreen.com/articles/aspects-in-astrology.

Aries 101: Everything you need to know about the kickstarter of the zodiac. (2021, March 26). Mindbodygreen. https://www.mindbodygreen.com/articles/aries-sign-101

Aries traits. (2021, October 4). GaneshaSpeaks. https://www.ganeshaspeaks.com/zodiac-signs/aries/traits/

Astrogle. (2009, September 6). FAQs about combust planets and their effects. Vedic Astrology & Ayurveda. https://www.astrogle.com/astrology/faqs-about-combust-planets-and-their-effects.html

Astrologernyc. (n.d.). Livejournal.com. https://astrology8.livejournal.com/1513.html

Beare, K. (2007, May 2). Zodiac signs and the words that describe them. ThoughtCo. https://www.thoughtco.com/zodiac-personality-4122956

Brennan, C. (n.d.). The planetary joys and the origins of the significations of the houses and triplicities. Hellenisticastrology.com. https://www.hellenisticastrology.com/the-planetary-joys.pdf

Broadwater, A. (2023, February 13). Mental restriction can be a major roadblock for intuitive eating – here's what helps. Well+Good. https://www.wellandgood.com/mental-restriction/

Brown, M. (2021a, October 11). A guide to air signs: Gemini, Libra, and Aquarius. InStyle. https://www.instyle.com/lifestyle/astrology/air-signs

Brown, M. (2021b, November 17). A guide to fire signs: Aries, Leo, and Sagittarius. InStyle. https://www.instyle.com/lifestyle/astrology/fire-signs

Brown, M. (2022, May 25). What each zodiac sign can expect while Mars is in Aries. Yahoo Life.

Bunch, E. (2020, January 21). The zodiac wheel is divided by extroverted and introverted energy – here's what it means for you. Well+Good. https://www.wellandgood.com/polarity-in-astrology/

Campbell, S. (2022, June 7). StyleCaster. StyleCaster. https://stylecaster.com/body-parts-zodiac/

Campbell, S. (2022, September 16). What does retrograde mean? How each planet's retrograde affects you. StyleCaster. https://stylecaster.com/feature/what-does-retrograde-mean-1134829/

Dictionary.com. (2022, January 21). Zodiac signs: Learn the names, symbols, and more! Dictionary.com. https://www.dictionary.com/e/horoscope-meaning/

Ep. 145 Transcript: The Origins of Horary Astrology. (2022, December 29). The Astrology Podcast. https://theastrologypodcast.com/transcripts/ep-145-transcript-the-origins-of-horary-astrology/

Finding the answers with Horary astrology. (2009, November 19). WellBeing Magazine. https://www.wellbeing.com.au/mind-spirit/Finding-the-answers-with-Horary-astrology.html

Getting started with horary astrology. (2018, October 5). Soul Friend Astrology. https://soulfriendastrology.com/2018/10/04/entries-into-horary-astrology/

Grabianowski, E. (2005, May 26). What Is Astrology? HowStuffWorks. https://entertainment.howstuffworks.com/horoscopes-astrology/question749.htm

Horary: Where is it? by Deborah Houlding. (n.d.). Skyscript.co.uk. https://www.skyscript.co.uk/wit.html

Houlding, D. (n.d.). Skyscript: Horary Love Charts. Skyscript.co.uk. https://www.skyscript.co.uk/relationships.html

Houlding, Deborah. n.d. "An Introduction to Aspects and Chart Shaping in Natal Astrology by Nicholas Campion." Skyscript.co.uk. . https://www.skyscript.co.uk/aspects2.html.

How to thrive as A water sign (looking at you, Cancer, Scorpio & Pisces). (2021, August 5). Mindbodygreen. https://www.mindbodygreen.com/articles/water-signs

How to thrive as an air sign (shoutout Gemini, Libra & Aquarius). (2021, September 13). Mindbodygreen. https://www.mindbodygreen.com/articles/air-signs

Ht, P. L. C., & More, R. (2022, March 3). What Is Horary Astrology? Complete Beginner's Guide. LoveToKnow. https://horoscopes.lovetoknow.com/astrology-basics/what-is-horary-astrology-complete-beginners-guide

Johnson, S. (n.d.). The essentials of essential dignities. Seeingwithstars.net.

Kahn, Nina. 2019. "What Conjunction, Trine, Square, Opposition, and Sextile Mean in Astrology & Birth Charts." Bustle. January 26, 2019. https://www.bustle.com/life/what-conjunction-trine-square-opposition-sextile-mean-in-astrology-birth-charts-13108526.

Katee, A. (2023, January 7). The 4 essential dignities of planets in astrology the keys to understanding your strengths and weaknesses. Well+Good. https://www.wellandgood.com/essential-dignities-planet-astrology/

Kelly, A. (2018, February 2). The personality of a Cancer, explained. Allure. https://www.allure.com/story/cancer-zodiac-sign-personality-traits

Libra zodiac sign: Symbols. (2019, June 18). Cafeastrology.com; Cafe Astrology .com. https://cafeastrology.com/libra-symbols.html

Mahtani, N. (2021, March 15). Horary Astrology Is Like a Q&A Session About Your Chart – Here's What To Know About it. Well+Good. https://www.wellandgood.com/horary-astrology/

Miller, K. (2019, July 20). What it means if you're A cardinal sign in astrology, according to experts. Women's Health. https://www.womenshealthmag.com/life/a28280252/cardinal-signs/

Miller, K. (2020, October 29). The zodiac's fire signs: Aries, Leo, and Sagittarius personality traits, explained by astrologers. Women's Health. https://www.womenshealthmag.com/life/a34329807/fire-signs-zodiac-traits/

Muniz, H. (n.d.). The 7 fundamental Cancer traits and what they mean for you. Prepscholar.com. https://blog.prepscholar.com/cancer-traits-personality

New insights into Mutual Reception. (2016, November 1). Sky Writer. https://skywriter.wordpress.com/2016/11/01/new-insights-into-mutual-reception/

Padmadeo, B. B. (n.d.). Astroturf. The Pioneer. https://www.dailypioneer.com/2017/sunday-edition/astroturf--the-precision-of-horary-astrology.html

Padmadeo, B. B. (n.d.). Astroturf. The Pioneer. https://www.dailypioneer.com/2017/sunday-edition/astroturf--the-precision-of-horary-astrology.html

Robinson, K. (2022, June 9). Decans (Decantes): Definition, Zodiac Signs, How to Find. Astrology.Com. https://www.astrology.com/article/decans-astrology/

Rose, K. (2020, August 22). What does the Aries symbol & glyph mean? YourTango. https://www.yourtango.com/2020336399/aries-symbol-zodiac-sign-glyphs-meanings

Rose, K. (2021, April 9). What does the Capricorn symbol & glyph mean? YourTango. https://www.yourtango.com/2020336299/capricorn-symbol-zodiac-sign-glyphs-meanings

Rose, M. (2022, August 17). StyleCaster. StyleCaster. https://stylecaster.com/different-types-of-each-zodiac-sign/

Rose, M. (2022a, December 29). Air signs, explained: Here's what it means to be a Gemini, Libra, or Aquarius. Glamour. https://www.glamour.com/story/zodiac-air-signs

Rose, M. (2022b, December 29). Earth signs, explained: Here's what it means to be a Taurus, Virgo, or Capricorn. Glamour. https://www.glamour.com/story/zodiac-earth-signs

Ross, H., Clarke, J., Young, E., & Bishop, K. (2018, December 18). What is my ruling planet, according to the zodiac, and what does it mean for me? Repeller. https://repeller.com/ruling-planets-and-what-they-mean-for-you-according-to-the-zodiac/

Sam, T. +., & Wander, T. (2021, June 7). What Are The 12 Houses In Astrology - . Two Wander x Elysium Rituals. https://www.twowander.com/blog/what-are-the-12-houses-astrology

Sam, T. +., & Wander, T. (2022, August 15). How To Read A Horary Astrology Chart - . Two Wander x Elysium Rituals.

https://www.twowander.com/blog/how-to-read-a-horary-astrology-chart

Sam, T. +., & Wander, T. (2022, February 7). Planetary dignities and joys -. Two Wander x Elysium Rituals. https://www.twowander.com/blog/planetary-dignities-and-joys

Sidharth, A. (2016, February 29). Horary astrology Hindu traditional system. The Astrology Online | Best Astrologer in India, Online Astrologer in India, KP Experts in India; Astrologer Sidharth. https://theastrologyonline.com/horary-astrology/

Sloan, E. (2021, October 16). Here's what the modality of your zodiac sign actually means, according to an astrologer. Well+Good. https://www.wellandgood.com/modality-astrology/

Spanner, H. (2023, January 4). Retrograde motion of the planets: Everything you need to know. BBC Science Focus Magazine. https://www.sciencefocus.com/space/retrograde/

Stardust, L. (2020a, March 12). Cardinal signs: The CEOs of your group chat. Cosmopolitan. https://www.cosmopolitan.com/lifestyle/a31434873/cardinal-signs-zodiac-astrology-meaning/

Stardust, L. (2020b, August 12). Everything you need to know about earth signs. Cosmopolitan. https://www.cosmopolitan.com/lifestyle/a33588028/earth-signs-astrology/

Stardust, L. (2021, October 15). Introduction to Horary Astrology: What Is It and How to Use It. Astrology.Com. https://www.astrology.com/article/what-is-horary-astrology/

Stardust, L. (2021, October 15). Introduction to Horary Astrology: What Is It and How to Use It. Astrology.Com. https://www.astrology.com/article/what-is-horary-astrology/

Stardust, L. (2021, October 15). Introduction to horary astrology: What is it and how to use it. Yahoo Life. https://www.yahoo.com/lifestyle/introduction-horary-astrology-235556300.html

Stardust, L. (2021, October 15). Introduction to horary astrology: What is it and how to use it. Yahoo Life. https://www.yahoo.com/lifestyle/introduction-horary-astrology-235556300.html?guccounter=1&guce_referrer=aHR0cHM6Ly93d3cuZ29vZ2xlLmNvbVbS8&guce_referrer_sig=AQAAADqJUemWCHLj9rVLm09sQ2l6nkP1vHgARcd4VQ_da5MxxoZ9g153UVQc1gDQj-4ABeWWfPZdZ_K-QAh08kG77IOb2Ccm5cFZWbWrnS-gbkyAWlj1I-zIrGKBsP6TCnytlUcvUUnY6OYBX91jUxue4zDji1gJTJLqwVOWv0d56MLI

Surtees, K. (2018, May 28). What is horary astrology? We take an in-depth look at the planets. WellBeing Magazine. https://www.wellbeing.com.au/mind-spirit/astrology/what-is-horary-astrology-we-take-an-in-depth-look-at-the-planets.html

Surtees, K. (2018, May 28). What is horary astrology? We take an in-depth look at the planets. WellBeing Magazine. https://www.wellbeing.com.au/mind-spirit/astrology/what-is-horary-astrology-we-take-an-in-depth-look-at-the-planets.html

Surtees, Kelly. 2018. "What Is Horary Astrology? We Take an in-Depth Look at the Planets." WellBeing Magazine. May 28, 2018. https://www.wellbeing.com.au/mind-spirit/astrology/what-is-horary-astrology-we-take-an-in-depth-look-at-the-planets.html.

Tarot.com Staff. (2017, February 9). Your Zodiac Sign's Power Color. Tarot.Com. https://www.tarot.com/astrology/zodiac-sign-colors

The 12 Houses of Astrology - The Astrological Houses and Your Natal Chart. (2020, August 14). Labyrinthos. https://labyrinthos.co/blogs/astrology-horoscope-zodiac-signs/the-12-houses-of-astrology-the-astrological-houses-and-your-natal-chart

The 12 zodiac signs: Traits, meanings, symbols, colors, and more! (n.d.). Tarot.com. https://www.tarot.com/astrology/zodiac

The Astrology Dictionary. (2012, July 24). The Astrology Dictionary. https://theastrologydictionary.com/d/decans/

The astrology dictionary. (2012, September 12). The Astrology Dictionary. http://theastrologydictionary.com/j/joys/

The Axis In Astrology – Ac, Ic, Dc And Mc. (2021, January 14). Star Sign Style. https://starsignstyle.com/astrology-axis-points-four-angles-explained/

Thiessen, A. (2017, November 2). The ASCENDANT and DESCENDANT Axis - . Canary Quill Astrology. http://www.canaryquillastrology.com/articles/2017/9/26/the-ascendant-and-descendant-axis

Thomas, Kyle. 2021. "Your Guide to Planetary Aspects." Cosmopolitan. August 18, 2021. https://www.cosmopolitan.com/lifestyle/a37341996/astrology-aspects-list/.

Time Nomad. 2019. "Minor Astrological Aspects and the Domain of Magic." Time Nomad. May 30, 2019. https://timenomad.app/posts/astrology/philosophy/2019/05/30/minor-aspects-domain-of-magic.html.

TIMESOFINDIA.COM. (2021, August 16). What does the symbol of each zodiac sign mean? Times of India. https://timesofindia.indiatimes.com/life-style/relationships/love-sex/what-does-the-symbol-of-each-zodiac-sign-mean/photostory/85349448.cms?picid=85349511

Transits: Predictions, Dates and Timings. (n.d.). Astrosage.com. https://www.astrosage.com/transits/

Wroskopos's blog. (2010, February 13). Wroskopos's Blog. https://wroskopos.wordpress.com/2010/02/13/starting-with-horary-the-basic-steps

www.ingramcontent.com/pod-product-compliance
Lightning Source LLC
Chambersburg PA
CBHW051850160426
43209CB00006B/1239